YOUTH WORK IN THE CHURCH

YOUTH WORK
IN THE CHURCH

By

NEVIN C. HARNER

GUIDES TO CHRISTIAN LEADERSHIP
PAUL H. VIETH, *Editor*

ABINGDON PRESS
NEW YORK ● NASHVILLE

YOUTH WORK IN THE CHURCH

Copyright MCMXLII by Whitmore & Stone

Library of Congress Catalog Card Number: 42-5462

Ω

SET UP, PRINTED, AND BOUND BY THE
PARTHENON PRESS, AT NASHVILLE,
TENNESSEE, UNITED STATES OF AMERICA

EDITOR'S INTRODUCTION

THE ABILITY to hold its youth is almost universally accepted as a test of the vitality of a church. Similarly, when the qualifications of a man for minister of a church are under consideration, his appeal to young people will be given a very high rating. If not considered of first importance, this qualification will be given a rating which is at least a close second to his ability in the pulpit.

This high regard for youth is based on sound considerations. If the church's message is to be effective in the world, it should have an early and important place in growing Christian character. If in fact there is to be a church tomorrow, then there must be young people in the church today. If the church is to respond to the challenges of the world with buoyancy and vigor, then it must have in its membership those who are accustomed so to respond to life.

The appeal of religion is not foreign to youth. This has been proved by youth's response in every age, including our own. The difference between a church which is blessed with large numbers of youth as active participants in its work and one which has lost its young people must therefore be one of approach and method on the part of those who bear the responsibility for youth leadership.

There is wide recognition of the need for youth to have a place of its very own in the church. But this must not be carried to an extent which separates youth from the larger whole which is the *Church*. To plan and carry out a youth program which escapes these two extremes, yet enables young people to find themselves really at home in their own organizations and also in the church as a whole, requires the best thought and effort of every minister as well as of the lay leaders of youth in the church.

Within the youth program of the church there are further problems which must be solved. How, for example, shall we plan for graded departments, morning and evening programs, without destroying the essential unity of the church experience of the young person? How shall we provide for many persons a leadership experience without having many churches of youth instead of one?

This book is addressed to the general problem of youth in the church as well as to the more specific problems arising within the youth program, such as those outlined above. The author, the Reverend Nevin C. Harner, Ph.D., is professor of religious education at Lancaster Theological Seminary. This consideration of youth work in the church is a worthy companion volume to his earlier book, *The Educational Work of the Church,* and carries out the implications of the latter as applied to work with the age group from twelve to twenty-four.

PAUL H. VIETH

PREFACE

UNTIL RECENTLY it was the fashion to assert glibly that the hope of the Church, of the nation, and of the world was in youth. Oppressed, perhaps, by our own sense of failure, we turned longingly to the next generation as the long-awaited Messiah that should lead us into the Promised Land. With the wistful confidence that a miracle was about to be wrought before our eyes, we gave ourselves to work with youth.

Then came the second World War with the incredible events leading up to it, and the optimism of this belief was rudely challenged. For we have been forced to witness millions of young people turning nationalistic overnight, and outdoing many of their elders in some unlovely traits which we thought humanity had outgrown. Surveying this scene, we can scarcely help asking: Why should we bother with youth, if this is what they are?

But these same facts are capable of a quite different and more convincing interpretation. They show beyond any doubt—do they not?—how enthusiastically youth will espouse a cause beyond themselves and sacrifice their very lives for it. They show also how readily youth can be molded either for good or for ill. We must not permit ourselves, therefore, to be betrayed into an unreasoning despair. If we ever hoped that youth by themselves would save the Church, or the nation, or the world, we were of course merely deceiving ourselves. But young people and adults working together in the spirit of Jesus of Nazareth—that is a different matter! In such *co-operation* lies a chief promise for a better day. Today more than ever it is essential that youth work in the church be done wisely and devotedly.

The discussion which follows in these pages attempts to

see the local church's program for youth in its whole range and scope. It is not concerned primarily with the church school, nor the young people's society, nor with the place of youth in congregational worship. Rather it endeavors to visualize in unified fashion all that a given church can do with and for those of its membership who are no longer children and not yet adults.

Acknowledgment is gladly made of the many courtesies received in the preparation of this manuscript. I am indebted to the following for permission to quote materials copyrighted by them: *The Christian Century*, the International Council of Religious Education, the Pilgrim Press, the American Academy of Political and Social Science, and the D. Appleton-Century Company.

Unnamed throughout the text are the following individuals from widely scattered localities who have kindly allowed me to use their unpublished researches or accounts of youth work: G. J. Bartholomew, G. H. Gebhardt, Mrs. J. D. Banks, H. E. Pearson, S. E. Mackey, H. E. Best, D. F. Singley, E. P. Hovey, J. A. Wenner, M. G. Wagner, G. A. Shults, P. Nagy, Jr., W. F. Lehman, A. R. Bodmer, Miss M. R. Lawson, T. G. Maughlin, and F. D. Wentzel.

The Reverend Fred D. Wentzel surveyed the outline of these chapters, and made suggestions which have materially enriched the scope of the treatment. Dr. Paul H. Vieth has been an invaluable counselor from first to last in the planning and writing of the manuscript. His rich training and experience have found their way at many points into the finished text.

To these and to many others with whom I have worked and from whom I have learned I desire to express my sincere thanks.   N. C. H.

CONTENTS

9

I

YOUTH CONFRONT THE CHURCH

THE CONSIDERATION OF youth work in the church rightly begins with the young people themselves. From coast to coast, at work and play and study, they are our chief concern. Students of the problem agree that there are in the United States upwards of twenty million young people between the ages of sixteen and twenty-four. To this number must be added—roughly speaking—five million more between the ages of twelve and fourteen, because these, too, are "young people" as the term is commonly used in Christian education circles. Twenty-five million youth or more, looking to church and synagogue for spiritual guidance!

It would be hard to imagine a more fruitful field for Christian service. Can the Church win and hold these young people—for their sakes? As they stand in a chaotic present and face toward an uncertain future, they desperately need the support of Christian beliefs and the guidance of Christian standards. Here, at our very doors, is a missionary field of the first magnitude. Can the Church win them and hold them—for its own sake? Its immediate future, at least, is in their hands. If it can reach them, it is safe. If it cannot, it is doomed to sure decline. Can the Church win them and hold them—for the nation's sake? The conviction is growing upon many thoughtful observers that there is no hope for democracy apart from a living faith in God. No

11

conceivable·amount of bombers and tanks will be able to guarantee the future of a democracy whose citizens have lost that which alone gives worth to every human being—namely, the belief that each man is a child of God. Will America's citizens tomorrow have such a belief?

It is with questions such as these that youth confront the Church. The first sure step along the road to an answer is a study of these young people themselves.

WHO ARE THESE YOUNG PEOPLE?

We are in a much better position to answer this question today than we were even five years ago. For one thing, adolescent psychology has made some rather significant strides during this period. For another, a major survey of American youth has been completed in recent years, putting in our hands a wealth of trustworthy information. The answer to our question can perhaps best be given in the form of a series of statements:

1. *These young people are in many respects like all other young people in every age and place.*

It is wholesome to remind ourselves that we today are disturbed about virtually the same traits of youth as have disturbed adults as long as there have been youth and adults. An interesting exercise in this connection is to try to assign a date to the following quotation from a sermon: "It is too true, frightfully, miserably true, that there is not the same reverence for parents as there was a generation back; that the children break loose from their parents, spend their parents' money, choose their own road in life, their own politics, their own religion, alas! too often, for themselves; that young people presume to do and say a hundred things which they would not have dreamed in old times." This sounds as though it might have been said last Sunday from some American pulpit. As a matter of fact, it was preached by Charles Kingsley, and recorded in a book published in 1858.[1]

2. *These young people are not as sharply distinct as we have thought from the children below them and the adults above them.*

It has been our custom to think of adolescence as a separate period of life, a time of "storm and stress" during which old personality-outlines were broken up and new ones formed almost overnight. It now seems that this notion will bear a grain of salt. Adolescence is, of course, a time of marked change; but the changes do not seem quite so marked as we once thought they were, and they may not be due primarily to the causes which we once held responsible.

Professor H. S. Dimock has probably done as much to correct our thinking in this regard as any other person. He undertook a most careful study of two hundred boys who were twelve to fourteen years of age when the study began. He followed them through a two-year period—that is to say, through the years of puberty which have been supposed to be the most changeful period of life. He did find some rather striking changes. For example, the amount of time spent per week in clubs, Scout troops, weekday meetings of church school classes, and the like declined on an average from 2.0 hours at age twelve to .2 hours at age sixteen.[2] On the other hand, the much discussed religious awakening which has been supposed to accompany these years failed to make an appearance in his study, at least so far as religious ideas and knowledge are concerned. The average scores on a test of religious thinking for the successive years were as follows: age twelve, 115; age thirteen, 125; age fourteen, 127; age fif-

teen, 125; age sixteen, 125.[3]   In corroboration of this point
may be cited the far-reaching statement of E. T. Clark in his
book *The Psychology of Religious Awakening* to the effect
that only 7 per cent of two thousand persons studied testified
to having had an experience of "conversion." [4]   It looks very
much as though there is nothing in the nature of human
nature itself through the 'teens that points an individual ir-
resistibly towards a dramatic conversion experience.   If
such an experience comes, it is most likely because people
expect it of him rather than because of any changes within
the individual himself.

This opens for us the general question, What are the chief
causes of such shifts in personality make-up as do take place
during the period of puberty?   Do these causes lie largely
within the boy himself and the changes which are occurring
there, or do they lie primarily in the outer world and the
changing relationship of the boy to that world?   Professor
Dimock's studies make him lean toward the latter point of
view.   Such shifts as take place in the adolescent's ways of
feeling and acting may, he suggests, be traceable primarily
to the expanding social world of the adolescent.[5]   Month by
month he spends ever more time outside his home in travel,
work, and other community contacts.   He comes in touch
with new standards of living which may not agree with
those of his home, new responsibilities, new types of people,
conditions which were a year ago unknown to him.   It is
these which tend to make him a somewhat different person,
and not chiefly some mysterious alchemy within his own
body.   The outcome of the whole study is the proposal,
made in the last sentence of the book describing it, that
there might be some gain in declaring a moratorium for a
while on the word "adolescence." [6]

It would be a mistake to follow this line of reasoning too far. Adolescence is truly one of the crucial periods of life. But it is also true that today's youth are yesterday's children and tomorrow's adults, and not a separate order of beings from another planet.

3. *These young people are proportionately fewer in number than formerly.*

In 1870 there were 537 young people fifteen to twenty-four years of age to every thousand older persons twenty-five to sixty-four years of age in the United States. By 1930 there were only 389.[7] Unless things take a different turn in the near future, those who have a flair for statistics predict that the number of youth in our country will reach its maximum around the year 1944, after which it will decline.[8] This means, among other things, that youth's commodity-value—so to speak—is increasing. The Church must be more zealous than ever before to win young people, for the very reason that there will be fewer of them.

The situation, so far as numbers go, is complicated by the fact that our young people are not distributed impartially through all sections of the country. For example, in 1930 there were only 292 young people to every thousand older persons in the state of California; in South Carolina there were almost twice that number, or 595.[9] By and large this works out to the disadvantage of our youth, inasmuch as the national areas with the most children and young people are the areas with the smallest income—and hence least able to give them the schooling and the care they need. The Northeast has only 30 per cent of the nation's children of the ages five to seventeen, and 43 per cent of the nation's income. Unfair as it may seem, the Southeast has 24 per cent of the nation's children, and only 10 per cent of the nation's income.[10]

A further fact, equally challenging in its implications, is that uniformly throughout the nation there are fewer children and young people in cities than on the farms.[11] The agricultural sections of our country are struggling under more than their share of the burden of rearing a generation of healthy, intelligent, upright youth. In some respects they are peculiarly fitted to carry this burden; in other respects not. During the depression many thousands of young people who in better times would have made their ambitious way to the city remained on the farms, thus piling the burden still higher. It is reckoned that there were a million more young people on the farms in 1935 than there were in 1930—and there were more in 1930 than agriculture needed.[12] The meaning of all this for the Church—if we have eyes to see—is that its treasures of men and money should be opened generously to the churches in those areas, mostly rural, where youth are most numerous. And for the workers with youth in such areas, who ofttimes must worry along with threadbare equipment and heart-breaking discouragements, there is at least the satisfaction of knowing that they hold a place of strategic importance to the Church of the future.

4. *These young people are, in many respects, more fortunate than any other young people who ever lived.*

A contributor to a recent symposium by sociologists on American youth sums them up as follows: "The prospective heirs of this American heritage are, despite some vicissitudes, the most intensively nurtured group of comparable size in all recorded time. They are bigger, heavier, stronger, healthier, wealthier, and more colorful than any generation which has gone before them. They are better fed, better housed, better dressed, better educated and more sophisticated than any of their predecessors, and they are the first adolescent Americans to be called collectively 'Youth.' " [13] All of these hopeful considerations should be borne in mind, as we turn now to the other side of the picture.

5. *These young people are "up against it" in a host of ways.*

They face difficulties, deprivations, and temptations whose combined effect may be little short of tragic. Let us pass over the ever-present threat of war and international collapse, and look only at those peacetime difficulties which confront them in season and out.

Many of our youth are "up against it" in the matter of employment. There is some little disagreement as to how many of our American youth are seeking work and finding none. A middle-of-the-road estimate, formed before our vast program of rearming was begun, states that of every ten young people in our country two are in school, two are home-makers or employed part time, four are employed full time, and two are unemployed. [14] During the second half of 1934 and the whole of 1935 the United States Employment Service received 1,883,000 applications from young people under twenty-one. Of these applicants 44 per cent were placed, which was a smaller percentage than obtained in any other age group. [15] The statistics bearing on this point can be heaped mountain high, and they all tell the same tragic story of wasted man power and woman power and of deterioration of the Almighty's most precious gift to this earth—fresh, new personalities. To point the same truth once again, in 1930 there were eleven million young people gainfully employed in our country; in 1935 this number had fallen to less than eight million. [16] What of the other three million? Is it any wonder that, when the Maryland study asked youth what personal problems gave them most concern, two-thirds mentioned economic security? [17]

The mere listing of unemployment statistics, however, does not tell the whole story. Many of the young people who have found employment are receiving wages too small to enable them to live in the present or plan for the future as they would like. Many also—far too many—are working at something different from that upon which they had set their hearts. In one city a thousand young people were questioned, and almost three-fourths said this was true in their cases.[18] One student of the matter has estimated that of the young people who turned their backs on school in 1936 about 400,000 would have liked to enter the professions, about 200,000 tried to do so, and about 87,500 achieved their ambitions.[19]

Many of our young people are "up against it" in the matter of the establishment of a home, and the relation between the sexes generally. It was estimated around 1936 that the number of delayed marriages in our country owing to the depression reached the sad total of a million and a half.[20] This fact, plus the automobile, and the cocktail bar, and the motion picture, and the pulp magazines, and a little chaos in notions of right and wrong, may carry some serious consequences in its train. The actual facts are not pleasant to recite, but the Church must reckon with them. The illegitimacy rate in America has risen since the first World War. In 1931 it had reached the proportion of 34 in every thousand births.[21] One of the best-informed youth leaders in the country conducted an investigation among 1,800 typical high school youth. He found that 29 per cent of the boys and 20 per cent of the girls had by their own admission seriously violated the Christian standards of sexual morality.[22]

Many young people are "up against it" also in the matter of recreation. In a special study of young people in a midwestern city one-fourth named recreation as the hardest problem they have to solve.[23]   In the suburbs of a certain eastern city a group of young people charged that drinking places outnumber churches two to one, commercial amusement places four to one, and playgrounds eight to one; and that in short in this city it is easier for young people to locate a place in which to drink than a place in which to play games.[24]   It should be clear that social and religious agencies have only scratched the surface of this problem of providing facilities for wholesome recreation.   The very careful study made in the state of Maryland turned up the fact that roughly speaking three-fourths of the young people of that state held membership in no clubs whatsoever.[25]   How long will it be until the Church realizes fully its obligation in this field, and faces it squarely?

In the light of such disclosures is it any wonder that a certain life insurance company had to reject in 1936 almost three times as many applicants under thirty because of the use of alcohol as in 1932—an alarming increase in the short span of four years? [26]   And is it any wonder that the nineteen- and twenty-year-olds outnumber any other two-year group in the prisons of our country? [27]   (To keep the record straight, and to scotch any needless fears, it should be said that there is no clear case at the moment for an increase in the delinquency rate, and there are some indications to the contrary.) [28]

Many young people are "up against it" in their relationship with their parents. From time immemorial, of course, there has been a measure of tension between the two generations—both in the home and elsewhere.   It is never easy for young people to imagine how things look to their parents, and it is no easier for parents to remember accurately how things looked to them in their youth. But there is some reason for believing that this misunderstanding is a little sharper than usual in our day. Society has changed with such incredible speed during the past quarter of a century that young people face a host of problems which their parents never knew, and they face the old problems in a new setting. Furthermore, young people are being trained nowadays to think for themselves, whereas many parents inherit the notion from an earlier day that young people's thinking should be done for them.

At all events—whatever the causes may be—this tension between the generations seems to be upon us. If it were not so, why should 1,968 high school seniors out of a total of 5,000 check positively the statement in a questionnaire: "I feel my parents try to run my life"? [29]

In the light of the foregoing we may attempt a summary picture of the chief problems perplexing youth. Perhaps as good a clue as any for this purpose is to be found in the responses of 1,200 young people, divided equally among the seventh and eighth grades, ninth to twelfth grades, the college years, and an employed group eighteen years of age and over. For the junior high school group it was the area of family relationships that concerned them most deeply. For the senior high school and employed groups it was the area of friendships. For the college group it was the area of mental and emotional health.[30]

On the surface youth are a rather happy-go-lucky lot. Probe a little deeper and you find many a worry and anxiety. One investigator in his contacts with five thousand high school youth found that the problems which tormented them most were fear and anxiety.[31]   These two words are strange companions of youth, but companions they are!

6. *These young people possess a rather high degree of moral and religious idealism.*

No portrait of modern American youth would be complete without this observation.   Whether young people ride in chariots, buggies, automobiles, or airplanes, they are always and forever dreamers of dreams.   This is not to imply that young people are innately better than children or adults, or that there is any magical flowering of idealism on a certain birthday.   A sufficient explanation may probably be found in the fact that they are old enough to be aware of the ancient ills of human society, and not old enough to have learned from bitter experience how stubbornly these ills resist human efforts to change them.

Nothing could illustrate better this ageless idealism of youth than the remarks of three modern high school students. For all we know, they speak the latest slang and wear the latest clothes and perpetrate the latest and most ungodly swing music, but this is what they said: "I hope to bring about the reform of all corruption in politics."   "I have the ambition of wiping every gangster and thief off the face of the earth."   "I have seen and heard of so much suffering that every thought that I have is leading me on to offer my services to the human race. . . . . I feel that I can and must take a medical course if there is a way at all." [32]

Nor are we to think that young people who will say this sort of thing are merely a handful of overpious exceptions. The United States Office of Education disposed of such a notion in one of the studies which it made.   One-half of the young people who were questioned revealed personal ambitions of a truly idealistic nature, and indicated furthermore that they had actually taken part in religious or social work.[33] These are the youth whom the Church must reach.

How Do They Feel Toward the Church and Religion?

On this point the Maryland study, to which reference has already been made, affords the most help; and the evidence is by and large rather reassuring. The facts which stand out above all others are that among the more than thirteen thousand representative young people studied three out of every four counted themselves members of some church, and six out of seven had been to church at least once during the year past.[34] These are high percentages. Even if they include a great number who are nominal members only, they still tell of a Church with considerable vitality and with a very real ability to hold young people. As we would expect, the Roman Catholic record is materially better than the Protestant record—at least in these outer measures of piety. Of the young people whose parents were Catholic 93 per cent regarded themselves as church members; of those whose parents were Protestant 69 per cent so regarded themselves.[35] Again, as we would expect, the Catholic record is the better of the two at the point of church attendance. Of the young people whose parents were Catholic 75 per cent reported that they attended church regularly once a week; the comparable figure for the youth of Protestant parentage is 39 per cent.[36] Taken all in all, the Maryland figures do not corroborate the usual picture of wayward and godless youth, and a dead or dying Church.

What lies back of this encouraging percentage of church affiliation and church attendance on the part of youth? The answer we would like to give is that youth find the ministrations of the Church indispensable for their souls' well-being.

No doubt this answer contains part of the truth, but scarcely the whole truth. A more prosaic answer is given by a contemporary sociologist in an analysis of why youth affiliate with the Church. Some of the reasons which he lists are: because everyone else does it; because of the wishes of parents; because of the opportunities for self-display which the Church and its auxiliaries afford; and because of the desire for social fellowship. Meanwhile, he says, strong emotional ties are being woven back and forth between the young person and the Church which tend to bind him throughout his life.[37]

We have, then, in the Maryland findings some ground for hope; and yet it would be a mistake to jump to overoptimistic conclusions concerning youth's relation to the Church. Probably a good many of the Maryland young people "go through the motions," and that is about all. We would be in error if we were to picture the great majority of American youth as being in the grip of an overpowering interest in religion and the Church.

If evidence for this is needed, it can readily be found in the responses of four thousand young people who were asked to check the questions which interested or concerned them from a long list covering all the major areas of life. As it turned out, the number of checks in the religious area was lower than in any other section.[38] Out of the four thousand, only 555 checked a question having to do with the nature of God; only 146 felt impelled to check a question having to do with the purpose of the Church.[39]

One more piece of evidence may be cited. In a recent article a university professor describes his attempt to sound out about eight hundred students of his institution on their attitudes toward religion and the Church. The students had before them a number of statements whose content ranged all the way from deep, unwavering appreciation of the Church at one end to absolute contempt at the other. The professor reports that such statements as the following were checked most often: "I am careless about religion and church relationships, but I would not like to see my attitude become general." "I believe in the church and its teachings because I have been accustomed to them since I was a child." "I believe in what the church teaches but with mental reservations." As he rightly observes, these attitudes are just a shade better than absolute neutrality regarding the Church.[40] Such replies are on the side of the angels, but barely so! They are scarcely the stuff out of which a strong Church can be built.

These are the young people who will be the leaders of our political, economic, and social life tomorrow. These are the youth whom the Church must reach.

How Does the Church Feel Toward Them?

This question, the complement of the preceding one, is hard to answer. There are differences among denominations, among churches in a single denomination, and even among the members of a given church in this matter of attitudes toward youth.

By and large the Church has lavished much sympathetic attention upon youth, in recent years particularly. It has borne them in mind in the buildings which it has constructed; it has made provision for them in its denominational and interdenominational budgets; it has supplied them with youth secretaries, youth hymnals, youth quarterlies, and a wide variety of splendid printed materials; it has spent thousands of dollars on youth camps; it has sponsored a nation-wide Christian youth movement under the "Christian Youth Building a New World" program; it has given them a share in its ecumenical conferences, and even promoted one ecumenical conference for them specifically. This is a record to which it can point with pride and satisfaction.

If the Church has failed at all with youth, it has not been so much at the point of material provision for youth work and programs, but rather in the more intangible realm of its feeling toward young people. The crucial question is, Has the Church always been as sympathetic, as understanding, as tolerant as it might have been toward youth? It is not the easiest task in the world to maintain these attitudes toward youth, but youth is still one of the members of the body of Christ, and as such must not be despised. The church that despises it is starting to dig its own grave. Several years ago publication was given to a striking letter from a leader of a large Protestant denomination. This most significant document reads in part as follows:

I was startled recently when I came across in my file an article by Reinhold Niebuhr on "The Youth Movement of Germany" (*The Christian Century,* November 1, 1923). Remembering the present situation in Germany, how startling is Niebuhr's description of the German youth of 1923: "Very critical of the nation, it regards narrow patriotism as a challenge to its ideals of fellowship and brotherhood . . . . looks toward a new community of peoples in Europe . . . . many definitely pacifistic, but even among those who are not committed on the war issue there is nevertheless a wholesome freedom from the national prejudices and racial animosities which animate many of their elders . . . . seek the elimination of all distinctions of race and class." And much more to the same effect.

What was the attitude of the church in Germany? Youth felt that the church was literally without sympathy because of its "narrow pietism and barren intellectualism," and that it was lacking in social realism and "morbidly self-centered."

I cannot but believe that the story of the German youth movement might have been different had the church not been introvert, if it had been willing to harbor the spirit of moral adventure and with youth seek a new world. What has happened is mordantly described by Mr. Henry Canby, the literary critic: "Europe displays the extraordinary and unhappy phenomenon of a debacle of the youth movement as bad as the ending of the most unfortunate crusade." *It can happen here.*[41]

This letter deserves to be read and reread by all who work with young people, and by all who love both youth and the Church.

THE CHURCH'S STRATEGY WITH YOUTH

We are now ready for the inevitable question, What can the Church do to win and hold its young people? Our concern for the moment is not with exact methods, programs, and tricks of the trade. Rather we must here at the outset go beneath these practical devices to the basic question, What shall be the Church's strategy in its dealings with youth? Young people being what they are, how can the Church approach them best? What shall be "the grand strategy" upon which it will rely chiefly in its efforts to win youth—for their sakes, for its own sake, and for the world's sake? Perhaps a helpful way of dealing with this question is to identify and weigh two contrasting strategies which can be used and are actually being used now by various branches of the Church.

The first may be put in these words: *In its efforts to win youth the Church ought to concentrate upon the weaving of emotional ties which will bind youth to itself so tightly that nothing which life can bring will break those ties.* Probably the most consistent exponent of this strategy over the years has been the Roman Catholic Church, although many Protestant denominations have employed it in varying degrees. Its essentials can be put quite simply. The child must be got young (compare the oft-quoted statement that the Roman Catholic Church wants a child until he is seven, and does not care who has him thereafter); then by constant contact with the Church, by oft-repeated suggestion, by beautiful ritual and captivating symbolism, by constant appeals that touch the heartstrings, the ties are woven between the Church and youth as a spider spins his web from point to point until at last the youth is bound body and soul to the Church. The Bible verse which best describes this strategy is the familiar "Train up a child in the way he should go; and when he is old, he will not depart from it."

The other strategy is markedly different. It might be put in these words: *The Church ought to concentrate in its efforts to win youth upon satisfying the life-needs of youth so completely as to become indispensable to youth.* The Christian education movement has rather consistently been an exponent of this strategy. Here the starting point is to ask, What do youth need? Do they need guidance to find their way through the maze of problems listed in the fore part of this chapter? Very well; we shall try to give it to them. We shall endeavor to preach sermons, some of which at least will give youth specific help on the problems of life-investment, the establishment of a home, the use of leisure time, and the like. We shall bring the resources of the gospel to bear on these life-needs as directly as we possibly can. Similarly, we shall try to make our church school program relate directly to these life-needs, ethical and religious, of youth. And what else do youth need? Do they need an outlook upon life, a religious faith which will steady them, sober them, and save them—a few things that they can count on, a few things that they can live for and die by? Very well; through worship and study and personal contact we shall endeavor to supply this need. Do they need opportunities for wholesome recreation, and is there no place in the community where these opportunities can be provided? Very well; we shall try to provide them through the Church. Do they need a new social structure in which to work out their lives? Very well; the Church will identify itself in all reasonable ways with the struggle for such a new order, and will do it openly so that youth can see it so doing, and will challenge youth to give themselves to the struggle with all the idealism they can muster. All this the Church will do, first, because youth needs it; and, secondly, because the Church dares to hope that this is the best way to win youth's allegiance. If it can come to mean so much to youth that youth cannot do without it, then the future of youth in the Church is assured. The Bible verses which best describe this strategy are the affectionate words of our Lord, "Feed my lambs," "Feed my sheep."

These are the two strategies which are before the Church in all its dealings with youth. Some interesting contrasts can be set up between the two. The former makes its appeal primarily in the realm of the emotions, the latter primarily in the realm of the intellect and the will. The former tends toward great assurance in matters of doctrine; the latter, while remaining loyal to the core of Christian truth, is alive to developments in science or philosophy, and encourages youth to make full use of their own God-given intelligence. The former is more likely to be sensitive to fine points of ritual and doctrine; the latter is more likely to be ethically and socially sensitive. The former leans in the direction of high church, the latter low. The former is likely to be Church-centered, the latter Kingdom-centered. The former faces toward the past with its wealth of tradition and its firmly established dogma and ritual; the latter faces toward the present scene with its kaleidoscopic pattern of problems and toward the longed-for future. The former makes for an old Church and an old religion; the latter makes for a youthful Church and a youthful religion.

Which of these two strategies is the more likely to win and hold youth? The answer is not easy to find, because the evidence is confusing. On the one hand is the undoubted success which the Roman Catholic Church has had with its young people—recall the data of the Maryland study—as well as some of the Protestant denominations which have proceeded chiefly along this line. On the other hand are the many young people who have been left cold by the former strategy, but won by the latter. The "Christian Youth Building a New World" movement, which has cut across some forty denominations and become the very bread of life to thousands of young people, is evidence for the latter strategy. Which shall it be?

Perhaps the best answer at which we can arrive on the basis of the evidence we now have is something like the following: *The former strategy is the surer one with most of the people most of the time. However, it stands to lose heavily at some important salients along the line of attack.*

It stands to lose heavily with the more brilliant intellectually among our American youth. The population of our colleges and universities is a case in point. Someday many of them are almost sure to turn against its hesitancy in accepting new truth, and that will be a sad day for the Church when they do so. Even now we are losing all too many of our finest college youth—a loss which we can by no means afford.

The former strategy stands to lose heavily also with the more sensitive ethically among our youth. Sooner or later they are almost bound to feel that it makes too much of fine points of ritual and dogma, and too little of the great matters of personal morality and social justice which mean life or death to thousands of human spirits. When this happens, they are likely to turn their backs upon the Church and find an outlet for their energies in co-operative societies, peace movements, and other "secular" agencies.

Further, the former strategy stands to lose heavily with the more needy physically among our youth. They will be content with it and with the Church which employs it so long as they are not too hungry, nor too much in need of a job, nor too tragically haunted by the specter of war and destruction. But if and when these actual physical deprivations lift their ugly heads, the danger is that they will look with bitterness upon a Church which has been able to do nothing more vital for them than to bind them emotionally to an ancient ritual and a time-honored dogma, no matter how beautiful the ritual or how true the dogma. This is not alarmist theory, but bitter fact. Youth have done this by the thousands in Russia, in Germany, in Spain, and in Mexico.

Up to a certain point the Church can and should follow both of these strategies; but sooner or later it must decide which one is to be central. If the preceding paragraphs are true, *it is the second strategy, not the first, which deserves to be central.* In the long run—not the short run, but the long run—the future lies with that Church which will so completely satisfy the deepest life-needs of youth as to make itself indispensable to them.

II

SIX BASIC NEEDS OF YOUTH

SOONER OR LATER in our consideration of youth work in the church we must look carefully at problems of organization and method; but first we need to go a little deeper into the needs of youth. Before we consider *how* to teach and *how* to organize, we must fix clearly in our minds *what* it is we want to teach and *what* we want to accomplish through our organization. For after all, method and organization are mere instruments in our hands through which we hope to touch for good the lives of our young people.

In the preceding chapter a number of the needs of youth were suggested. It is not possible to enter into all of these minutely; we must choose the most important. The question is, Which are the most important? Of all that have been listed or can be listed, which are the six that are crucial to the spiritual well-being of youth? Which come closest home to the young people whom we know and with whom we work? Different people will of course give differing answers to this question. However, there will probably be wide agreement that young people between the ages of twelve and twenty-four need to make the following six "discoveries":

1. They need to find God.
2. They need to find themselves.
3. They need to find a life work
4. They need to find a life mate.

31

5. They need to find society—and their relationship to it.

6. They need to find the Christian society, the Church—and their relationship to it.

Let us look at each of these in turn. What are the chief needs of youth in each of these areas? What should be the chief points of emphasis for the Church as it endeavors to meet these needs? What dangers are to be avoided? What in general shall be the Church's approach to each of these areas of basic need?

The Need for a Vital Christian Faith

Was there ever a time when this need was more desperate than today? And, on the other hand, was there ever a time when it was harder for young people to achieve such a living faith than today? It is not only that the tragedy and the chaos of world conditions makes faith in the Christian God extremely difficult. This would be obstacle enough, if it were all—but it is not all! A further obstacle to Christian faith is the fact that the air is so full of conflicting ideas and systems of thought. Fascism and Nazism proclaim a national God who cares for a chosen people. Communism proclaims no God at all. Even the theologians dispute among themselves as to who God is, and where he is, and how he works among men. What shall a young person believe? Yet another obstacle to Christian faith is the general unsettling of men's minds which science has brought about. There was a time when it was a simple matter to discover what to believe. All that was needed was to consult an infallible Bible, or an infallible Church, and the trick was done. But for many of our young people today an easy solution such as this is out of the question. They have been taught from childhood in the public schools to think for themselves, and to take little or nothing on authority. In the long run this will doubtless make for a faith based on sure foundations, but during this period of transition for many there seem to be no foundations at all. Still another obstacle is the fact that our young people have grown up in a world that is largely secularized—which means a world in which God is referred to casually or incidentally, if at all. They do not hear him spoken of in their schools to any extent. Many of them do not hear him spoken of in their homes. He seems far distant from the everyday world of work and play. Why should they believe in him—really believe in him? In the face of all this, we of the Church have let them down by failing to give them any sound theological training during their childhood years in the church school. Is it not so? Some of their teachers have been none too sure of God themselves—perhaps this is the chief difficulty.

The foregoing paragraph paints a rather gloomy picture. When we turn to the young people themselves, do they fit this picture? In considerable measure they do. What we actually find in them is some true Christian piety, a good bit of muddy thinking about God, and a fair amount of plain, out-and-out indifference.

For example, the nation-wide weekly *Scholastic* made a survey recently in the high schools of our country to discover how much vitality there is in the religious faith of our high school students. More than six thousand questionnaires were returned. The conclusion was that for 85 per cent of these young people religion had less meaning than it had for their parents.[1] This is progress in the wrong direction.

Another indication of how the land lies is to be found in a thesis the purpose of which was to investigate the vitality and practical worth of the religious experience of church

youth. One hundred questionnaires were returned by young
people fifteen to twenty-four years of age, all of them members of church youth groups, eighty-seven members of the
church itself. The following answers are significant in the
present connection:

Almost unanimously they agreed with statements of a general
nature:
    93 of the 100 checked positively "Religion is very real to me."
    89 checked positively "Prayer gives me strength for living."
    94 checked positively "I have accepted Jesus as my example,
        hero, pattern in life."
When it came to indicating specific meanings which their
religious faith should have for their daily lives, they were much
less certain:
    23 marked as true "I do not see that religion has anything
        to do with boy-girl relations."
    87 marked as true "Most young people choose their vocation
        without considering the plan of God."
    10 marked as true "My life-work need have nothing to do
        with making the world more Christian."
    Only 25 said they held regular private devotions.
    70 gave no reply to "Religion affects my leisure-time activities
        in such ways as the following: . . . ."

This is sufficient to indicate the magnitude of the task
which the Church faces in cultivating a living faith among
its youth. What now shall the Church do? How shall it
move to meet this challenge? All that we can hope to do
here is to suggest a few general guiding principles.

As a first important step, *the adult workers with youth
must be sure in what and in whom they themselves believe.*
If they are not sure, they must do the studying, and the reading, and the thinking, and the praying, and the living necessary to achieve this assurance. The adult workers with youth

in a given church or a number of churches combined might well devote a number of conferences to the earnest discussion of such questions as, who is God? who is Jesus? what is the Bible? what is the Church? what can prayer accomplish? There are some excellent books available which might serve as the basis for such discussions.[2]

What the adult worker himself believes is of central importance in Christian education—much more so than we have been wont to acknowledge in recent years. Strangely enough, it is the emphasis on democracy in teaching that has led us into this error. We have been very zealous to encourage youth to do their own thinking and arrive at their own faith; we have shied off from anything that looked like imposition of our own ideas or indoctrination in our own faith. This in the by and large has been wholesome, but it has betrayed us into the fallacy that a teacher or counselor dare not "let himself go" in religious faith and enthusiasm; or, if he does, he must studiously hide this fact from his young people. This is a tragic fallacy. An adult worker may believe something with all his heart, and may earnestly desire that those whom he teaches will come to the same belief, and at the same time refrain from thrusting this belief down the throats of his students. Positive belief does not necessarily imply dogmatism, nor indoctrination, nor any of the other ugly things we wish to avoid. On the contrary, young people, while remaining free to exercise their own minds to the full, have the eternal right to live in intimate fellowship with older persons who have achieved a rich, sure faith in their own lives and are willing to testify to that faith whenever the occasion demands it.

In the second place, *the Church must formulate a careful strategy for dealing with those youth who have begun to question the older forms of Christian belief.* There is no universally acceptable solution to this problem, for the very reason that some adults will not welcome these questionings of youth, while others will. The former group, while remaining true to what they conscientiously believe, can render a real service to youth by respecting their thoughts and questions and refraining from all condemnation. They can also concentrate attention on some high Christian doctrines which remain far above the battle, as it were. The goodness and the greatness of God, the spiritual and moral grandeur of Jesus' life and death, the infinite worth of every human being as a child of God, the faith that there is a divine plan for society and for individual lives—all of these are untouched by any of the sure findings of science. For the latter group some such strategy as the following may be suggested:

1. Teach positively, not negatively. In other words, stress what we can and do believe, rather than what we can no longer hold. Too much has been made of the things that must be given up, and not enough of the things that abide. We would have a rich Christian faith if only these three things remained: Jesus is the finest we know; God is like him; it is our business to be like him. That would be enough to live by and die by.

2. Deal with controversial doctrinal issues principally on one of two conditions: (a) if a question has been openly raised by the group, or by someone in the group; (b) if the teacher feels that the issue will be raised for some of his young people in the near future under less favorable circumstances. If a teacher knows that some of his young people will soon come under the influence of a college professor, for example, who takes delight in shocking youth, he may well decide to

raise some questions himself so as to make sure that they will be handled sympathetically.

3. Handle controversial issues frequently in individual conferences. This procedure is particularly to be recommended when a question is vital to only one or two in the group, and has not yet come over the horizon for the remainder.

4. Use what may be called a "two-way strategy." The heart of this strategy consists in pointing out that there are two ways of answering almost every theological question, and that there are equally good people on both sides. This approach, while encouraging youth to take their stand definitely in one of the ways, leaves them tolerant and charitable toward those who take the other way. It saves them from narrow self-righteousness, and it leaves them free to worship side by side with their parents and others who may take the other way.

5. Use the educational method. That is to say, begin with people where they are, and take them gradually and lovingly to where they ought to be.

A final word in this discussion of a vital faith for youth may well be concerned with the troublesome matter of prayer, especially private prayer. There are many indications that for countless young people prayer is by no means a life-giving and life-supporting experience.

One way of assisting them to make wise use of a daily period of private prayer is to acquaint them with the devotional manuals available, of which *The Upper Room*[3] is probably the most widely used. Furthermore they need some specific guidance in how to spend five or ten or fifteen minutes in daily meditation. For example, we may offer them a concrete list of steps to be followed, a sort of spiritual road map

for their journey Godward.   The following has the merit of
being easily remembered, in that the first letters spell the
word "true."

Think about God.   Allow your mind to dwell deliberately
and at some length upon the goodness and greatness of God,
who is over all and in all and through all.

Remember all He has done for you.   Call to mind in gratitude
the many divine mercies which have flowed ceaselessly into your
life during the hours and the years that are past.

Undertake to do something specific for Him.   Settle upon
some concrete and homely way in which you can fit your little
life into the ongoing, mighty purposes of God.

Entrust yourself to His care.   Put your heart and mind at rest
in the sure knowledge that all of life is in God's hands, and that
neither life nor death nor any possible happening can separate
you from His love.

Perhaps if we could encourage our youth to make an honest
trial of such a devotional plan day by day over a period of
years, God himself would assist them to a vital faith.

The Need for Self-Understanding

This is a need which can be overlooked all too easily.   It
has not fallen within the scope of Christian education, as we
have usually defined that term.   We have seen our responsibility to teach the Bible, to teach Christian doctrine, to
teach Christian ethics; but to help young people to understand themselves—that scarcely belonged to Christian education, as we have thought of it.

Do young people themselves sense this need?   If one can
judge by the eagerness with which they respond to an opportunity for gaining some understanding of themselves, the
answer is Yes.   In the leadership training curriculum of the
International Council of Religious Education there is a

course entitled "Understanding Ourselves," designed primarily for youth. About fifteen young people along with one or two adults enrolled for this course on the opening night of a community school. They were given a list of possible topics and asked to leave the space before a topic blank if they were not interested in it, to check it if they would like to see it discussed, and to double-check it if they would like very much to see it discussed. The first figure in each parenthesis indicates the number of checks; the second figure the number of double checks. It is revealing to note both the range and the extent of their interest in these questions:

(7-1)   1. Do we inherit bad temper, dishonesty, fear of snakes, insanity, etc. from our parents?

(5-2)   2. Are there any inborn differences in character or temperament between boys and girls?

(10-1) 3. How are Christian habits, such as truthfulness, kindness, etc., acquired?

(7-3)   4. How can undesirable habits, such as bad temper, gossiping, smoking, be changed?

(6-3)   5. What are the basic drives or interests or desires of life, which make us do all the things we do from buying a new dress to going to church?

(6-2)   6. Ofttimes life does not give us the things we want. Is it true that the source of most nervousness, shyness, queerness is right here?

(8-0)   7. What are the strange tricks we play on ourselves and others to get what we want, when life denies us our desires?

(5-3)   8. Why do we feel the way we do toward Negroes, Hitler, the church, communists, the flag, etc.?

(8-0)   9. What are the changes, physical and emotional, which take place between 13 and 16? How do they affect the way a person feels and looks at life?

(3-5) 10. How do the following home conditions affect the growth of Christian personality: Being an only child? The oldest child? The youngest child? Being loved too much? Being disciplined too severely? Misunderstandings between parents? Having a more popular brother or sister?

(5-4) 11. What do young people and their parents disagree over chiefly? What can be done about it?

(7-1) 12. Why do some people get along well in school, and others poorly? Is it solely a matter of differences in intelligence?

(4-7) 13. Why is it so hard to "go against the gang"? What should a person do when his ideals about drinking, for example, differ from those of the group he runs with?

(3-5) 14. How can we tell what is right and wrong about smoking, drinking, petting, militarism, etc.? Are our consciences always right?

(6-6) 15. What things ought a person know about himself in choosing a vocation? What shall one do if he can't get a job year after year?

(7-1) 16. How can a person make friends? What kind of person has the most friends?

(2-8) 17. How should boys and girls treat one another? What should they do on a date? What physical intimacies, if any, are wholesome? At what age should a person settle down to a "steady"? Is dancing good or bad?

(8-2) 18. What good can religion do a growing perosnality? Prayer? Church attendance? Bible reading?

What can the Church do to meet this need of youth for self-understanding? How shall it approach this relatively new task? There are two principal ways, the one working with groups, the other with individuals. In the first place, *we can provide units of study in practical psychology in church school classes and societies, as well as community*

training schools and camps. These courses should be in-
tensely practical; they should be built around the questions
and perplexities of young people themselves; and they should
be taught by someone who knows psychology. It is not
enough to set young people wondering about themselves;
many of them are doing too much of such aimless wondering
already. They cannot open the doors into a fuller self-
understanding merely by groping with their bare hands in
the dark. They need keys, and keys that fit. In this instance,
the keys consist of a few basic concepts in the psychology of
personality. A certain young man in a summer camp troubled
everyone with his loud boisterousness, and probably troubled
himself as well. He did not know why he was boisterous.
The door to an understanding of himself at that point was
locked tight. In all probability his boisterousness could be
traced to the fact that he was an adopted child—a fact which
had been hid from him for several years. He did not know
that his foster-parents were not his real parents until some
children with children's cruelty cast it in his face one day at
school. The keys to unlock this door would run somewhat as
follows: our personalities are shaped largely in childhood;
we all want security; when we don't have it we sometimes
compensate for the lack of it by boisterousness. These keys
can be simply put—as can all the basic ideas of modern
psychology—but they are stock equipment for the teacher
who hopes to unlock the doors of self-understanding to youth.

The group approach, however, is not enough. It can
bring a large measure of self-acquaintance to those who do
not need it too badly, but those young people who are
laboring under real difficulties within the narrow confines
of their own lives cannot get the help they need in group
sessions and courses of study. In the second place, therefore,

*we can provide personal counseling, especially for the young
people who need self-understanding most urgently.* A later
chapter will give some further attention to this important
matter.

The Need for Christian Vocational Guidance

It might be supposed that this need was being met satis-
factorily—what with the rather extensive efforts along this
line of the public schools and other character-building agencies. However, it seems that the program of vocational guidance has not yet caught up with the need. This is indicated
by the fact that less than one-fourth of the young people
questioned in the Maryland study said they had been given
fairly adequate vocational guidance.[4] Of those who had
received such guidance and were now out of school, almost
three-fourths regarded it as of help to them.[5] Apparently
young people welcome vocational guidance, find it valuable
when they receive it, but are not getting as much of it as
they would like.

What are the particular points of need in this field today?
It goes without saying that the usual detailed study of self
and the detailed study of vocations and the matching of one
with the other will continue to be in demand. In addition
to this conventional program, are there any particular points
of need arising from the situation in which present-day
young people find themselves? A survey of the situation
suggests several.

*They need to be delivered from a concentration on white-
collar jobs.* This, of course, is easier said than done. As
long as professional and business positions are paid more
highly and honored more lavishly, young people will continue to set their hearts on them. The Maryland study

found that almost three-fourths of the young people wanted to go into white-collar jobs.[6] This figure includes far more than can ever hope to find such positions. It includes also some who are not intellectually fitted for such careers. All of this suggests that the Church may well counsel young people in the spirit of the Parable of the Talents, whose central teaching is that various grades of service are equal in God's sight, provided each man does his own best.

They need assistance in holding their lives together when the months go by and no jobs are found. This is a poignant need for thousands of present-day youth, varying of course in intensity from time to time. The Church is in a strategic position to meet this need. It cannot always find work for them, although it can do this in isolated cases. But it can equip them with avocations—hobbies and interests of many kinds—which will partially fill the vacuum left by unemployment. In its own life and work—its church school classes, clubs, and choirs—it can give lost youth a chance to make their lives count, and thus enable them to retain their individual sense of worth. And it can always surround them with a sympathetic Christian fellowship and inspire them with the Christian philosophy of the infinite value of each human being, employed or unemployed, which will help them to keep their chins up and their eyes toward the future.

They need to have the Christian vocational motive made clear and compelling. The word "Christian" was included here purposely. There is vocational guidance, and beyond that there is *Christian* vocational guidance. The Church has something to say to youth as they face their life careers which the public school or a guidance bureau cannot say explicitly and fully. It has a divine plan of life to hold before their eyes. It has the Christian ideal of service to throw into their calculations, as they try to find the niche in which they will spend their lives. It has all the needs of all mankind the world around to bring home to them. This is the unique task of the Church in vocational guidance. How much of the rest it does will depend upon what other agencies in the community are doing, but this is its own peculiar specialty.

What, now, can the Church do to meet these needs? In its church school classes and youth fellowships *it can offer the conventional type of vocational guidance through group study and interviews with individuals.* One church, for example, enlisted the help of a specialist from the public schools in outlining a program of vocational guidance for its youth of high school age. The project began with a study of the ethical and religious aspect of vocational choice—namely, the meaning of God's will for individual lives. It then moved on to the giving of a battery of tests, measuring interests, aptitudes, and emotional adjustment. Representatives of a number of professions were then invited to give the group the inside story of their several vocations. Medicine, the law, nursing, engineering, the ministry, aviation, and un-skilled labor were among those thus presented. This was followed by interviews between individual young people and representatives of the professions in which they thought they were interested.[7] Whether stock vocational guidance of this sort shall be given by a church, and how much of it is to be given, must be decided in the light of what other community agencies are doing.

Beyond this, there seem to be certain special obligations resting upon the Church. As suggested above, *it is the Church's special obligation to make vivid the appeal to a life of service.* One wise teacher helped his class of boys to construct a date-line after the H. G. Wells pattern which ran from prehistoric man to the events recorded in the morning newspaper. Under his guidance they saw that line making its precarious way painfully upward from chaos to order, from savagery to kindliness, from the law of the jungle to the law of love. They saw God brooding over this line, as it were, and working out his purposes in man and with man. And *from there* this teacher went to the matter of choosing a vocation. How could they fit their individual lives into that line? This is true Christian vocational guidance. Services of worship are needed also, preferably at the close of such a period of study, during which young people can feel deeply about, and perhaps dedicate themselves to, a life of service. In addition, there should be face-to-face contact with the dire needs of humanity at home and abroad, physical and spiritual, which then become the vivid backdrop before which Christian youth pause to choose their life-work.

The Church has a special obligation also to teach biography as a part of its program of vocational guidance. Young people see so much and hear so much of lives that are lived ignobly; they have a right to an acquaintance with some noble lives as part of their equipment for wise vocational choice. This should include some truly great biographies—from the Bible, from the history of missions, from the fields of art and science, and the like. But it should include as well some ordinary everyday people who lived happy and useful lives.

The Church has a special obligation to present the claims of professional Christian service. It is the local church and the youth program of the local church which alone can insure a never-failing supply of ministers, missionaries, and other full-time Christian workers. Conferences cannot achieve this end; nor can denominational colleges; nor can theological seminaries. A major share of the responsibility rests upon the local church. It will not, of course, tell youth that only in the ministry and kindred fields can one render Christian service, but it will hold up the vocations of the Church as splendid ways of investing the years of one's life. This challenge it will not hesitate to extend to the very best, the strongest, the keenest, the most popular young people within its fellowship.

Finally, *the Church has a special obligation to reach parents in the interests of wise vocational choice on the part of youth.* For often the well-meant but unwise urgings of fathers and mothers are a chief stumbling-block in youth's way. Of all the agencies which attempt vocational guidance the Church is best situated to reach the parents, for the Church has access to them as the public school, for example, does not. This places a special responsibility upon us, which we should gladly accept for youth's sake.

THE NEED FOR CHRISTIAN SEX EDUCATION

There can be no question as to the need of youth at this point. Many young people are caught in secret worries, tensions, and conflicts whose storm-center is sex. Many more are engaged in sexual conduct or misconduct which may effectually bar them and others from the abundant life. Meanwhile they find it extremely difficult to obtain reliable and wholesome information concerning this important phase of living. In the Maryland study only 30 per cent of the young people said they got their sex knowledge chiefly from parents and relatives; most of them got it from youth of their own age.[8]

We are not at a loss as to the questions which chiefly perplex youth in this regard. In a recent careful study young people in a number of different groups were given a chance to submit questions in this field. Among the fifteen problems raised most frequently, the one at the top of the list—as we might expect—had to do with petting. Three of the fifteen had to do with engagements—how long they should be, what physical intimacies are permissible, and how engagements can be broken off. Three others dealt with the troublesome problem of differences between two young people—differences in race, in religion, in age, in education—and how serious these differences are. Two of the fifteen concerned what might be called the etiquette of dating—girls making dates, picking up dates, and the like. Other problems figuring among the fifteen were the advisability of trial marriages, the nature of true love, and birth control.[9] These are some of the urgent questions on which young people need help. They look to the Church, as well as to other agencies, for such help.

The first question we must face, as we contemplate giving this help, concerns not the *how* but the *what* of Christian sex education. What do we want to teach in this field? What philosophy of sex is in best accord with sound psychology and the Christian view of life, as we understand them? To put it practically, what are the chief points we would like to get across to our young people? Perhaps the crucial ones are the following:

1. *That all questions of conduct between the sexes are to be decided not on the basis of momentary pleasure but on the basis of the ultimate well-being of all concerned.* This would seem to be a basic principle, and it would seem to be Christian. Asceticism is not Christian. To deny the existence of a God-given part of us, or to deny it expression under any and all circumstances, is surely pagan. Thoughtless indulgence is not Christian. To do whatever one pleases

whenever one pleases, regardless of the consequences, is surely pagan. But to meet every situation in life in the manner that promises to bring the most happiness to the most people in the long run—that *is* Christian! This principle has far-reaching implications for the way in which boys and girls should treat one another.

2. *That sex has no right to play as large a part in the lives of youth as it sometimes does.* Some young people, looking into their own lives around the age of sixteen or eighteen, might find half of their free thoughts devoted to sex, and half of their worries clustering around sex. But surely sex cannot be as important to life as that! Perhaps what looks to us to be sex interest is one-third unsatisfied curiosity. If the curiosity could be relieved, sex would shrink into its rightful place in life. Perhaps what looks to us to be sex interest is another third the effect of artificial stimulation by motion pictures, pulp magazines, and lurid conversation. If this could be stricken out, sex would shrink to its rightful place in life. This is a line of reasoning which seems perfectly true, and promises to be of real help to our young people.

3. *That restraint of the sex impulse is not necessarily harmful psychologically.* This is a point of the utmost importance, because young people are being told the opposite on every hand. There is no support from the science of psychology or from the experience of people for such a doctrine. Young people need to be informed clearly and unequivocally that it is not true. The truth of the matter is that there are conflicts and doubtless nervous breakdowns over sex, but that these are brought about not primarily by self-restraint but by self-condemnation and shame. This is a rather neat psychological point, but a highly important one. A person

who is hungry, but who for good and sufficient reasons declines to eat for a while, will not by the wildest stretch of the imagination undergo a nervous breakdown. He might, on the other hand, have a nervous breakdown if he had been taught from childhood that it was shameful to be hungry; that no decent or self-respecting person would ever admit to others or to himself that he was hungry. Apply this analogy to the field of sex, and the necessary distinction is made. It is not primarily what youth *do* about sex, but what they *feel* about sex that makes for mental health or its opposite. To say it differently, it is not *suppression,* the open-and-above-board restraining of an appetite, that does mental harm; it is *repression,* the guilt-ridden feeling that an appetite must be completely disowned, that does the harm. To sum it up, self-restraint is not always easy, but it is never necessarily harmful.

4. *That there are good and sound reasons for restraint of the sex impulse.* We have long been familiar with the negative reasons for such restraint—the danger of venereal infection, the possibility of bringing unwanted new life into the world, and the like. We are now able on the basis of modern research to adduce positive reasons, which strengthen the case materially. We can now say with considerable assurance that there is a greater chance for marital success and happiness to those who in the days before marriage have the strength and wholesomeness of personality to obey the time-honored Christian ideal concerning the relation between the sexes, and do so. A writer on this subject gathers up three separate researches, all of which point in the same direction. He cites the study of Hamilton, who made a comparison between men who had had no sex relations before marriage and men who had. Of the former, 57 per cent made a happy adjust-

ment in marriage; of the latter, 46 per cent. The comparable figures for women are 49 per cent and 37 per cent respectively. Next he gives the findings of Davis, who compared two groups of women—the one group happily adjusted in marriage, the other not. Of the former, 2.5 per cent had engaged in sex relations before marriage; of the latter, 15.2 per cent. To these he adds his own study of five hundred happily married couples and five hundred unhappily married. Of the former, 128 couples had anticipated the marriage ceremony; of the latter, 237.[10] These differences all run in the same direction. We owe it to young people to let them know this.

5. *That even minor physical intimacies need to be brought under definite control.* This is the difficult question of petting, which arises sooner or later in virtually every discussion of boy-girl relations. Some Christian counselors take the clear-cut position that there should be no intimacies whatsoever before engagement. Others in turn incline toward the position that certain minor intimacies are permissible and wholesome on condition that three very definite provisos are met. First, these intimacies must not have too much time devoted to them. There is a wide difference between a bit of physical closeness at the end of a happy evening of skating and two or three hours spent in a parked automobile. Secondly, these intimacies must stop short of the point where they demand further intimacies. This means that they must stop very short indeed. The only way of insuring this is to give young people a chance to work out for themselves a clearly Christian code of conduct before the date begins. There is a wide difference between a hug or a kiss and the various forms of "heavy petting." Thirdly, these intimacies are legitimate only between two young people who through

considerable acquaintance have come genuinely to know and care for each other. There is a wide difference between the kiss which seals an adolescent love affair and the promiscuous petting of a boy and a girl who met each other ten minutes ago. In the one case the intimacy is the expression and the carrier of a spiritual intimacy; in the other it is physical stimulation pure and simple. The position here being outlined can be summed up in the statement that it makes a great difference *how long, how far,* and *with how many* these minor physical intimacies are carried out. In all honesty, there is a good deal which can be said for this position. However, each worker with youth must make his own decision as to the stand he is going to take.

The foregoing has been an attempt to state a Christian philosophy of sex for youth, the *what* of sex education. There remains the *how* of such education. What shall be the nature of the Church's program in this field? This too can be cast in the form of a set of guiding principles.

1. *Sex education should not be attempted in a group unless certain important conditions can be fully met.* It is no light thing to attempt sex education in a church school class or young people's society. To begin with, the young people in the group—nine times out of ten—will approach the subject with so much misinformation and such twisted attitudes that they are not free to discuss the matter dispassionately as they would, say, the co-operative movement. This means that progress into the subject must be exceedingly slow and cautious—about three times as slow as the inexperienced teacher would think necessary. Then there are the parents and the rest of the church and community to be borne in mind. What will be their reaction to the rumor that such and such a youth group is talking sex in its regular

meetings? Finally, there are the qualifications of the counselor himself to be considered. Has he equipped himself for this important task of guidance by a painstaking study of the physiology and the psychology of sex? Is he himself emotionally unshackled so that he is free to discuss the subject with sufficient frankness to be helpful and without too much personal enjoyment of the discussion? In short, the youth groups in which anything more than a superficial discussion of boy-girl relationships can be safely undertaken are probably in the minority—at least for the present.

Having said this, we may add that where the young people are ready and the community willing and the counselor capable there is real gain in giving sex education in a group—even a mixed group. The very openness of this procedure puts sex on the same footing with other matters that are discussed openly. It is helpful to another boy to know that boy No. 1 has many of the same questions and anxieties that he has. It is helpful to girls to hear expressed the viewpoints of boys, and vice versa—all of course within the bounds of good taste. Sex education in a group, therefore, is either very good or very bad, depending upon the conditions under which it is done. Where it is attempted, it is probably best to make it as a rule a part of a larger study—biology, for example, or physiology, or hygiene, or human relationships, or Christian ethics. To say, "We are now going to have a six weeks' study of sex," merely serves to separate sex from the rest of life; and it has been separated too much and too long already.

2. *Much can be accomplished through personal interviews.* The trusted counselor will find young people seeking him out at the time of engagement, at the approach of a marriage, when a love affair goes wrong, and on other occasions.

It is his high privilege to make himself ready for these opportunities when they come.

3. *Much can be accomplished through carefully selected reading.* Each youth group might well place in its library such books as the following:

For the preadolescent intermediate: F. B. Strain, *Being Born* (D. Appleton-Century Company, 1937).

For the high school group and young people generally: R. E. Dickerson, *So Youth May Know* (Association Press, 1930).

For older young people: R. A. Burkhart, *From Friendship to Marriage* (Harper and Brothers, 1937).

For those married or about to be: M. J. Exner, *The Sexual Side of Marriage* (W. W. Norton and Company, 1932).

A bad book is worse that none at all. Most books written twenty years ago should be shunned, as should many books advertised through the mails. The ones listed above are scientifically and ethically sound.

4. *One of our best services to youth is to teach them what to do on a date, and to teach them to do it.* Many young people fall into unwholesome conduct, not because they are vicious, but because they know nothing else to do. Their repertoire of wholesome activities is simply too limited. If they do not know music, and do not enjoy art, and do not like to read, and have no handicraft skills, and possess no hobbies, and have never learned outdoor games and sports, it is little wonder if they make some mistakes in their associations with each other. The Church, therefore, can perform a real service to young people by giving them an opportunity to discuss ways of spending time on a date, and by actually giving them a chance to learn skills and hobbies of various sorts. In other words, some of our best sex education can be done without mentioning sex at all.

5. *Another splendid service to youth is to provide occasions under church auspices for wholesome association between the sexes.* We have no right to criticize young people for frequenting unsavory places, so long as we do nothing to provide something better. By providing something better, we choke out the worse, and we also set a pattern of happy association between the sexes with no self-reproaches the following day which will accompany our young people wherever they go. This too is good sex education without the mention of sex.

THE NEED FOR CHRISTIAN SOCIAL EDUCATION

It was said near the beginning of this chapter that young people need to find society and their own relationship to it. Do they really need this, or are we merely imagining that they do? If we are in doubt as to the answer, we have only to look across the seas. There we can witness millions of German youth, for example, giving themselves with reckless, joyous abandon to *a social goal.* To be sure, in the minds of many it is narrow, and even vicious in some particulars, but it is social nevertheless. It is something that concerns many people, and promises a better day for them. Perhaps there is something deep in youth which needs to find a social goal for which to live and die. And is there anything our hard-beset world needs more than a few million youth who will tackle its problems intelligently and self-sacrificially and in the Christian manner?

This, then, in brief is the case for Christian social education in our work with youth—it is sorely needed for the sake of both young people and society. To be sure, it should not be overdone. The Christian gospel is good news for both the individual and society, and these two sides of the gospel's meaning must always be kept in proper balance. In a young people's program—to be more specific—it would be a great pity if all of the time were spent on a study of co-operatives and none on a study of prayer, and it would be an equal pity if all of the time were spent on prayer and none on co-operatives.

There are those who feel that attention to social problems has been greatly overdone in some of our youth work in the churches, and in support of their contention they point a finger at the extremes to which certain young people have gone in speech and action on social issues. The conclusion they draw is that social problems have been stressed too much in our youth work. It may be so, but the exact opposite is possible—namely, that these excesses of young people came from too little rather than too much social education, and that the real need in church work with youth is a more thorough and a more Christian social education than we have ever had thus far. Certainly our young people themselves are hungry for help on more than one life-and-death issue.

Of what will this Christian social education consist? It will include, *first, a thoroughgoing study of God's will for human life* as we find it portrayed in the eighth century prophets, the Gospels, and elsewhere. It will start not with statistics, but with the Bible. What does God want individual men to become? What does God want mankind to become? What do we mean by the kingdom of God? What did Jesus mean when he used this phrase? What in our contemporary life is causing the heart of God to grieve? How would he want it changed? For this is *Christian* social education, and it should be different from a class in civics or sociology.

It will include, *second, a realistic study of urgent social problems.* Against the background of what we believe God's will to be, we must find out what the present situation is, and why it is as it is, and what it is doing to human beings, and what position a Christian should take concerning it. This requires facts, and more facts. What is the actual income of the average sharecropper? What is the real diplomatic history of Germany and Great Britain during the past twenty years? How many people are there to a square mile in Japan? What is the effect of alcohol upon the nervous system? Who owns and controls the chief newspapers of America? What is the true economic situation within Russia today? Our Christian social education of young people must take them deep into the most reliable sources of information we can discover.

It will include, *third, a careful examination of the role an individual Christian ought to play in society and of the role the Christian Church ought to play.* These two are not necessarily the same by any means. For example, it is perfectly in order for an individual Christian to join a given political party, but it is rarely in order for a denomination or a congregation to do so. In all probability a considerable part of the mistakes that have been made by socially minded Christians—and there have been some mistakes—were due simply to a failure to make this important distinction.

It will include, *fourth, actual participation in the struggle for a more Christian society.* This is the most difficult and at the same time the most essential step to take. If we stop short of this, we have cheated our young people. They have not found society and their relationship to it until they have actually done something heart-breaking or even back-breaking for the creation of a better world. No religious group has known this better than the Society of Friends. Through their work camps, their peace caravans, and their projects of relief to the needy throughout the world they have given hundreds of young people a chance not merely to be of service to others but to round out their own Christian social education.

THE NEED FOR ROOTAGE IN THE CHRISTIAN FELLOWSHIP

The Christian fellowship means, of course, the Church. It should require little argument to show that our young people need to be attached deeply and irrevocably to the Church. And probably we should have to admit that by and large we have done only a poor and bungling job of rooting our youth in this fellowship. The classic example of our failure is the case of the pastor who "rounded up" a group of his happy-go-lucky young people for presentation to the church officials. They were to "join the Church." As it happened, they were busy that evening with a dance.[11] Now that is no way to join the Church, the Body of Christ, the fellowship of Christians, the most glorious institution this world has ever seen.

What now shall we do to remedy the defect? Again, we must content ourselves for the moment with some guiding principles.

1. *We must give our young people a happy, rewarding experience in a church group of their own age and kind.* This may seem to be beside the point, but it is not. It is basic. How can they really belong to the local church and the Church Universal, unless they first belong to their own little church, their "ecclesiola," their own class or society or fellowship? This happy, rewarding experience should begin in earliest childhood and continue unbroken throughout life. It requires a joyous fellowship with parties and socials and fast friendships—but it requires something more and some-

thing more important! The *program* of their little group
from the kindergarten on must meet their deepest life-needs.
This is the first real step toward belonging to the Church.

2. *We must provide our youth many satisfying contacts
with the whole church body—in worship, in work, in play.*
This does not contradict the first point listed above, but
supplements it. A part of youth's church experience should
be with its own group, its little church; but another part
should be with the whole church. There should be some
worship with the church as a whole, the entire Christian fellowship. By the same token, there should be some *work*
with the congregation as a whole, the entire Christian fellowship. Joint congregational activities can be found in which
young and old will share alike. Also, there should be some
play with the congregation as a whole—two or three times a
year perhaps.

3. *Around the age of fourteen we should offer a thorough
course of study on the Church primarily, its history, its organization, its program, its worship.* This may conceivably
be done in the church school within the regular course of
study. Increasingly it is being done in a separate class,
a church membership class taught by the minister. Probably
the best plan of all is to do both. If the church school curriculum around this age can give careful attention to the life
of Christ and the history of the Church, these important
items can be marked "attended to" so far as the minister's
class is concerned, and he can concentrate upon a careful
study of the church's worship, its organization, its far-flung
program, the privileges and responsibilities of church membership, and the like. One year of thirty weekly sessions is
scarcely long enough for this separate class.

4. *We should induct our youth into complete church membership with the most stately and impressive ritual we can devise.* Some of the elements which enter into this memorable step in various churches are: a personal interview by the minister with each member of the class; a public meeting of the class with the church officials, parents, or even the entire membership, at which the class members give evidence of their knowledge as well as their Christian faith and purpose; a significant service at which the class members take the vows of Christian discipleship, and those who have gone before them renew their vows; and a first observance of the Lord's Supper, wherein the class commune as a body. Experiences such as these are not easily forgotten in a day or a month.

5. *We must not forget them thereafter but continue earnestly to solicit their full participation in the church's life.* For this more than mere invitation or scolding is required. Some ministers continue their church membership class at less frequent intervals, tapering it off gradually and thus continuing a personal touch with their youth. In churches not too small, a desirable plan is to make promotion into the Senior High School Department coincide with entering upon full church membership. Thus there is a place in the church's setup where the new church members are all together, and where pastor and lay workers can keep in touch with them. Further, the church worship including sermon can bear them and their deepest life-needs in mind; the church budget can be vividly interpreted to them for their hearty support; and the church's program can by special effort find abundant place for them with their many talents and their boundless energy.

To some of these matters we shall return in greater detail in later chapters. What we are attempting here is merely to draw a blueprint of what can be done by way of incorporating each successive group of wistful youth into the age-old Body of Christ.

III

THE PLACE OF YOUTH IN THE CHURCH

As WE THINK of the average church up and down America, how shall we picture the place of youth in it? Shall they have no special place at all, and be left merely to "tag along" in the way which their elders determine? Or shall they be given to stand at the center of the church's life—like Joseph's sheaf with all the other sheaves doing obeisance to it? What is their rightful place for their own good and for the good of the Church and the Kingdom? These are the questions to which we now address ourselves.

An Organization of Their Very Own

This would seem to deserve being the first part of our answer. They have a right to an organization of their very own. Just what it is need not matter so much, so long as they feel it to be their very own. And whether or not they feel it to be their very own depends only in part on the way it is set up. The organizational scheme may be letter-perfect, with youth officers and committees, a constitution, and all the recommended trimmings, and still the essential feeling of *ownership* on the part of the young people may be lacking. A certain youth group had a church school department which the director of religious education proudly thought was their very own. They had their own officers, considerable share—as he thought—in carrying out their own program,

61

and an adult counselor of the department who was trying his best to stay in the background. One day the president of the department came to see the director. He unwound himself to the full six feet four inches of height which he had attained during the last year or so, and announced that he and others would like to start a young people's society. When the director asked the inevitable "Why?" the president replied, "Because we want to have an organization of our own." There followed a conference far into the night between the director and the counselor of the department, during which ways and means were sought and found for allowing the young people to take the reins even more fully into their own hands. The point is that, after all, it is the way the youth feel about the matter that counts.

What shall this organization of their very own be? There is, of course, no one answer. The size of the congregation, the size of the church building, the traditions of the community, the overhead denominational program for youth— all of these help to determine what it shall be. All we can do here is to list some of the most likely possibilities—not necessarily in the order of their importance or value.

1. *One or two church school classes for youth.* This is the simplest organizational plan possible, and the one most likely to be followed in small churches in either city or country.

2. *A Sunday evening society or fellowship.* Commonly such a society or fellowship has existed alongside of and in addition to classes or departments for youth in the church school. We are not without instances now of something new—namely, the society or fellowship superseding the church school entirely so far as youth are concerned, and becoming the one center of youth work in the church. For

example, in a church noted for its success with youth there are now no Sunday morning church school classes for young people whatsoever except for the junior high school department and a class of young people who are in training for teaching work in the church school. The youth of the parish attend the morning church service in surprisingly large numbers. Then on Sunday afternoon and Sunday night the facilities of the church and the time of the pastor belong to the young people—six different groups of them. Properly speaking, all of these hold their educational programs on Sunday night. The afternoon of Sunday is devoted to preparation for the evening programs, plus various fellowship activities. On weekdays there are athletics, hobbies, parties, and the like. The church is open every day and all the time. Friday evening is reserved especially for the junior high school group, and Saturday evening for the high school age and above.[1]

This is an example of the Sunday evening society or fellowship becoming the all-inclusive youth organization of the church. In most communities for the present, however, it is doubtful whether a Sunday evening program will reach as many youth as the traditional church school program on Sunday morning.

3. *A special-interest group.* In some instances an organization built around a special interest, such as music or drama or missions, becomes the living heart of youth work in that church. By way of example, one minister testified that his young people's choir was the most live youth organization in his church, and did more than any other to hold his young people to the church and its purposes. In cases such as this, the special-interest organization may stretch its program to

include socials, periods of study, or worship services, until it is considerably more than a narrow special-interest group.

4. *A number of separate youth organizations.* In large churches, particularly city churches, the youth organizations tend to multiply until their name is legion. A good illustration of this tendency is contained in a study which a city church made several years ago of its youth between the ages of twelve and twenty-four. The findings in part were as follows:

53% of its youth of these ages were affiliated with the church in some way.

41% were moderately active church members.

30% were regular church school members.

9% of those of proper age belonged to the intermediate Christian Endeavor Society.

4% of those of proper age belonged to the senior Christian Endeavor Society.

14.5% of those of proper age were Boy Scouts.

16% of those of proper age were Girl Scouts.

22% were reached by church and church school.

6% were reached by three agencies.

.5% were reached by four agencies.

41% of the church members within this age range were not affiliated with any auxiliary organization in the church.[2]

This study reveals well certain ever-present dangers to which the youth work in large churches is subject. Clearly the minimum rather than the maximum number of youth organizations should be sought, and these should be tied together tightly either by a youth council or else by a congregational council in which all the auxiliaries of the parish are represented.

5. *A youth department in the church school as the all-inclusive youth organization of the church.* Probably for

many churches this may be held up as the ideal toward which we should strive in the immediate future. (It goes without saying that a single department can scarcely serve the whole age range of twelve to twenty-three, and several youth departments may be necessary.) In many instances everything that really needs to be done for and by youth within a given church can be done within the framework of a youth department of the church school. There can be study, and study of the problems that concern youth most deeply. There can be worship—all the separate worship that youth need. There can be fellowship. There can be activities of service. There can be due attention to drama. There can be youth officers, with an adult counselor designated by the school as a whole. If a Sunday evening meeting seems desirable, this organization can plan it and hold it.

And then, in proportion as the church school is tied in closely to the church, in proportion as it becomes the school of the church, this department becomes an unmistakable part of the church itself. It may even be called the Youth Fellowship of ————— Church, or the Youth Department of ————— Church. For most congregations whose buildings are large enough to permit one or more church school youth departments, this type of organization would seem therefore to be the most workable ideal for the years just ahead. It has much to recommend it, and only one serious drawback—namely, the danger that some church school officials will lay too heavy a guiding hand upon it.

The foregoing are some of the most common patterns which youth work in the local church is likely to take. We can scarcely leave this subject without paying some attention to the use which the church may make of the programs of the Boy Scouts, the Girl Scouts, 4-H Clubs, and the like.

These nation-wide agencies are in existence, ready and anxious to be used by churches. During 1939 almost one-tenth of all the Boy Scout troops in the country were under the sponsorship of one of our larger denominations.[3] The Boy Scouts of America have issued a manual entitled *The Scout Program in Protestant Churches* which gives detailed instructions for the closest possible alignment of Scouting with the purposes and program of the Church. Similarly, many Girl Scout and Camp Fire Girls units are attached to churches. The 4-H Club movement has had a rapid growth among rural youth, enrolling almost a million and a half boys and girls in 1939.[4] It too can be utilized by the Church. An account of several years ago tells how this movement was actually so used. In a certain county it was discovered that only 27 per cent of the rural youth were related to church or church school. The county farm agent, when approached, showed an extreme willingness to expand the "Heart" section of the 4-H program along any reasonable lines suggested by the ministers.[5] These are but scattered examples of the possibilities resident in nonchurch youth agencies.

Undoubtedly a fine service can be rendered to countless young people by the Church's sponsorship of programs such as these. In many instances this includes a missionary service—that is, it reaches boys and girls who do not belong to the church's fellowship but who live within sound of its bells. We should of course examine all such programs closely to see if they are calculated to promote the high spiritual ends which we set for our work with youth. If they include any features, such as an emphasis upon credits and awards, of which we do not wholly approve, we will endeavor to minimize those features. Furthermore, we do not want to multiply youth organizations unnecessarily. Every new youth agency should be put on the witness stand and made to prove its right to a place in our church's setup for youth. And finally the local units of these agencies should be correlated as closely as possible with the remainder of our youth program and with the work of the church as a whole.

AND YET A PART OF THE WHOLE CHURCH

This second heading completes the sentence which the first heading began, and a very necessary completion it is. The truth is that we face a dilemma in our youth work. We must have a separate organization for young people somewhere in every church, and yet we dare not have a separate organization. Nothing but harm can result from erecting a wall, or allowing one to be erected, between youth and the rest of the church.

The situation in this regard in many churches is far from a happy one. Young people often actually think more of a class, a department, or a society, than they do of the church. They may have their names on the church roll, to be sure, but their real membership—the membership that counts—is in one or more of these auxiliaries. We can never hope to develop good churchmen and churchwomen in this manner.

Furthermore, it is truly pathetic in many churches to discover the way youth feel toward adults, and vice versa. In a group of fine young people discussing youth work in the church one of the problems checked most frequently was, "How can young people and adults get along together better in the church?" In some churches the relationship between the two generations might be described as one of mutual disregard. In other churches there is active tension—over the breakage of chairs during an exuberant social, over the question of dancing in the church building or under church auspices, over the young people's interest in social issues which some of their elders do not share. In still other churches there is trustful fellowship between the two generations, and a sense of oneness in a common task.

Here, then, is our dilemma: Youth must have an organization of their very own, and at the same time they must feel that they are a true part of the church and their organization is a true part of it likewise. How shall we meet this dilemma? There appears to be no other way out but to give them an organization of their own, and then take great pains to tie it in to the rest of the church in every conceivable manner. Let us endeavor to set down some of the ways in which this tying-in can be done.

1. *Through common organization.* Somewhere in every church there is needed an organization which will see the life of that church as a whole, and plan for it in its entirety. It may be a board of Christian education, or it may be a congregational council, or it may be merely the official board of the church which adopts this as one of its major responsibilities. Every group and auxiliary, including those that have to do with youth, should be represented in this clearing-house.

Some congregations make it a point to include a certain number of younger men and women within the membership of the official board. This guarantees that the viewpoint of youth will be expressed, and further that there will be a never-ceasing supply of leaders for the church. One congregation has hit upon an interesting variation of this plan, which it feels is working with unusual success. The pastor writes of this plan in glowing words:

Ours is not, properly speaking, a junior official board, but a group of "associate officers" who meet with the regular official board and from whom vacancies are usually filled. There are six, elected each year according to their "interest." Most of them are younger men; three of the present six are single men. There is nothing to prevent our selection of a young woman for the position.

The values I see in our plan are: These men are tested as available timber for future officers; they learn the work and problems of the Church, locally and at large; they are prepared by their associate membership for fuller responsibilities later on, if they manifest interest, dependability, etc. All associate officers are placed upon the regular committees of the board, and share in the usual work of the other officers, including visitation, every-member canvass, and the like. They are usually selected from definite groups and organizations within the congregation, so that our board has at all times a full-rounded representation and expression of the various age groups and interest groups of the church.

We have had this plan working now about five years, and are well pleased with the results. Five of our present ordained officers have come up through associate membership. I should say that the attendance of the junior officers at the meetings compares very favorably with the attendance of the ordained officers.

It is safe to assume that such a plan as this, if honestly administered, would go far toward binding the young people closely within the larger church fellowship.

2. *Through common worship.* We have already spoken briefly of this point, and the chapter which follows will give it closer attention. Suffice it to say here that it is of the utmost importance that all youth in full church membership be present regularly in both body and spirit when the congregation worships. This requires careful planning of both service and sermon, and further a strict time limit on all separate young people's worship in church school or society. If these separate services are so lengthy or so elaborate as to make our

youth feel that they do not really need the church services, are we not actually inviting them to stay away?

3. *Through common work.* We do well to find as many things as possible which young people can do in common with those above them in age as well as with those below them in age. Youth and adults need to do things together in the church—many things. The young people will learn much from their elders, and the adults will find that their juniors are interested in something else than Hollywood and swing music. Similarly, young people need to do some things together with the children of the church. It is good for the children to see those who have reached the awe-inspiring age of seventeen or eighteen truly concerned with the things of the Kingdom, and it is good for the young people to get acquainted with the children whose teachers and guides they must soon become. The following is a very partial list of some joint activities—a hint merely of what can be done:

a) The every-member canvass (or whatever name is given to the annual effort to enlist the financial support of the church's membership) provides an admirable opportunity for youth and adults to collaborate helpfully. Imagine an equal number of young people and more seasoned workers meeting for the necessary preliminary training, and then going out two by two to lay the Christian cause upon the hearts of all the members of the church. (It goes without saying that each young person should contribute faithfully to the church's support himself, and thus enter into the common work.)

b) The preparation of special programs on missions, or stewardship, or world brotherhood, or for Children's Day, or Mother's Day offers youth a chance to work in company with both adults and children. Each age group can prepare and make its own special contribution to the joint program, according to its own interests and abilities.

c) A church-renovation or church-building program literally invites all ages to join in a common effort. Young people can assist in the preliminary planning, help with the publicity, present special programs, and make their own financial contribution to the enterprise which concerns all alike so deeply.

d) Ventures of social service, or of social reconstruction, demand the closest co-operation of youth and adults. Young people are eager to help refugees, or the unemployed, or to root out gambling, or to stave off the evils of war; but often the task is beyond them. The eagerness of youth plus the wisdom and experience of age makes a good combination.

e) A congregation-wide project represents the most ambitious plan for enlisting the combined efforts of all ages within the local Christian fellowship. In this plan the entire congregation, including all ages and all auxiliaries, concentrate their energies for perhaps a three months' period upon one central theme. It may be missionary work in China, or the Christian family, or the Bible, or the redemption of the surrounding community. Church services, church school, women's, men's, youth, and children's organizations revolve about this theme for a given period. The plan has been tried successfully in a number of churches. In order that youth may feel themselves truly a part of such a congregation-wide project they should in all fairness have a part not merely in the execution of it, but also in the planning of it.

4. *Through common play.* In all probability young people prefer to enjoy most of their good times in the absence of noisy youngsters as well as kill-joy oldsters, but several times a year there is a real place for congregational fellow-

ship with no age limits. This is truly "fellowship of reconciliation." Such possibilities as the following come readily
to mind:

a) The old-fashioned Sunday school picnic does not deserve
the premature death which it has suffered in many instances.
It was a time when parents and children, aunts and uncles,
neighbors and friends threw precaution to the winds in regard to both diet and exercise, and enjoyed themselves together. It still lingers in some places, particularly in rural
churches. Some city churches are reviving it; only it is no
longer a church school picnic, but rather a congregational
picnic—which is all to the good. If all ages are to attend, the
program will have to be carefully planned to include features
attractive to each age.

b) The winter congregational picnic is, it seems, a modern
invention. It is a good one. It is a true picnic, held in winter and indoors, and designed to be of interest to all ages.
It may come at the time of the annual congregational meeting, although not necessarily so.

c) Mother-daughter and father-son banquets afford excellent opportunities for bringing adults, youth, and children
together. By their very definition they include them all.
Again, young people will take a greater interest in these
events if they have a share in the planning and in the program. For sake of variety why not mother-son and father-
daughter banquets occasionally?

d) The entertainment of one group by another is a useful
way of bringing the two together. The young people can
prepare a "reception" to the adults, for example, and the
adults can return the favor.

5. *Through common discussion.* Talking things over
and out is one of the time-honored ways of removing and

preventing misunderstandings. But how often in the average church do young people and adults sit down together to discuss some of the matters which concern them both? A certain young people's fellowship was engaged over a series of Sunday evenings in a discussion of boy-girl relationships. It soon developed that one of the chief difficulties lay in the differences of opinion on such matters between the young people and their parents. Accordingly, the counselor devised a questionnaire which she asked some of the parents within the congregation to fill out. The questions in part ran as follows:

What time should boys and girls come home from parties and dates?

Do you leave your child alone when he or she brings a friend home, or do you stay with them?

Does the young person have a right to use the car for a date or going to a party? How often should he or she be given this privilege?

Do you give any guidance to your child concerning the persons he or she associates with? If your advice is not heeded, what do you do then?

What do you most approve of about the young people today?

What is your greatest criticism of the young people today?

The answers were carefully tabulated, and as a final step the parents were invited to meet with the young people at their regular Sunday evening meeting for a joint discussion of these problems. This would seem to be a useful method applicable not only to questions which arise in the home, but also to those which arise in the church. For this purpose there might well be occasional joint meetings of youth and adult church school classes and other groups. An excellent manual has recently been prepared for use in such discussions.[6]

6. *Through common overhead planning denominationally and interdenominationally.* In the very nature of the case those who are responsible for planning a youth program within an entire denomination or an even larger constituency are strongly tempted to see their task as a thing apart. The same is true for those who plan adult programs. When these separate plans percolate down into the local church they cannot help setting youth off to some degree from the rest of the church. A remedy is in sight if those who plan at the top will have regard to what others are doing and what the whole church is doing, and perhaps meet with others for joint planning. The United Christian Youth Movement and the United Christian Adult Movement, both sponsored by a number of denominations co-operatively, have much in common and were quite obviously designed with an eye upon one another. In a certain denomination the committee charged with drafting the youth topics for a year took into account the proposed study programs of the men's and women's organizations within their denomination in order that youth and adult groups in any given local church might suddenly find themselves considering much the same topics. In ways such as these those who plan at the top can make for understanding and fellowship at the bottom.

BUILDING A YEAR'S YOUTH PROGRAM

Our consideration of youth's place in the church has thus far had nothing at all to say about one crucial matter—namely, the actual content of a program for youth within the local church. This is not the place to discuss such a

program in detail, but it is a fitting place to try to picture
how it might be built.

A plan which seems to be winning increasing favor is to
outline the year's program for youth at *a retreat*—the name
is unfortunate, but the idea is sound—held during the
latter part of the summer before the active fall work begins. Let us endeavor to visualize such a retreat. It will
be held during the last of August, or the first week of September at the latest. The place, if in the city, will ideally
be a summer cottage belonging to one of the members of the
church and thrown open for this purpose. In the country,
the retreat may be held simply at a near-by home or else on
the church lawn. The church school teachers of young people's classes will be there, as well as youth spokesmen from
each such class or else officers and committee chairmen if
there is a church school youth department. In addition,
we shall find the officers and adult counselor of the youth
society or fellowship, if one is in existence, plus officers and
advisors of any other youth organizations in the congregation. We want every last phase of youth work in the church
to be represented, but we do not want an unwieldy group,
and—of particular importance—we prefer that adults be kept
in the minority. In all likelihood the minister will wish to
be present. A full day will be devoted to this retreat. The
forenoon will offer several hours for consistent work. The
afternoon will provide additional hours for finishing the task,
and also some games and a swim. Supper and a vesper service of consecration will round out the day.

What will be done at such a retreat? There will naturally
be great variety from church to church and from year to year,
and there is no thought at all that one step should follow
another with machinelike precision. Nevertheless, the gen-

eral order of the day's procedure may turn out somewhat as follows:

1. *The determination of the major emphases for the coming year.* In order to do this wisely, several things are necessary.

   a) *A consideration of what has been studied and done during the past year.* To this end several people will have been posted in advance to review briefly the past work of the youth groups within the church. What was studied in church school during the past year? What topics or problems were considered in the society? What has been done in the way of worship? Service? Fellowship? Dramatics? How have young people attended church? Have the intermediates lost interest, or the boys, or the young people who are out of school? As this proceeds, certain gaps may begin to make themselves felt. If it turns out that nothing has been done along the line of vocational guidance for a year or even longer, or that there has been no forthright study of the life of Christ for a considerable while, or that dramatization has been utterly neglected, or that the social program went to pieces, or that the high school boys have drifted away from the church—then we begin to see what needs to be done during the year ahead.

   b) *A consideration of what the respective groups are interested in.* Perhaps it was arranged several weeks previously to talk over in classes or youth fellowship what the group would like most to do in the coming year, and representatives of the groups are now ready to make their reports. Or it may even be that a check list was used to get a more accurate picture of interests and needs. The findings of this check list are now reported, and the high spots duly noted.

   c) *A consideration of what is happening in community, and world, and church.* Was there a strike within the bounds of the community recently, and did our young people manifest a real interest in it? If so, that fact is suggestive for our next year's program. Is there a war in progress which fills everyone with apprehension and uncertainty as to the stand a Christian ought to take? Is our local church celebrating an anniversary this year, with its inevitable recalling of the past history of the church and the denomination? Is our denomination in company with others observing Stewardship Year? These are but illustrations of the way in which program suggestions will emerge from a survey of what is going on around us.

d) *Now certain emphases ought to begin to stand out.* As the key persons at the retreat ponder the facts they have before them, and add thereto their own serious thought, they will find themselves saying, "In our youth work this year we must do this, and this, and this."

2. *The construction of tentative plans for getting these things done.* This is the second half of the task, and involves in turn certain general steps.

a) *Allocate tasks to the respective youth organizations.* In a small church simply organized this of course is unnecessary, but where there are several youth groups some convenient division of labor may be in order. For example, if some consistent Bible study has been agreed upon, the church school may be assigned that responsibility. If an emphasis upon worship and the cultivation of the devotional life is on the docket, or an informal discussion of certain life problems, the youth fellowship may seem the best place for that. And so on!

b) *Outline roughly the study program for the year.* What curriculum of study shall be followed in the church school? In the light of our emphases shall we follow the lesson series of our denomination, or choose our own units of study for a while? (A prospectus of the lessons for the year ahead can easily be procured for any series.) What shall we discuss in our youth fellowship? In the light of our emphases will it be better to follow one of the available sets of topics, or to construct our own? And so on through the other youth organizations, if any.

c) *Outline roughly the worship program for the year.* What would we like our "separate" services of worship to be like? Wherein have we fallen short? What should we do differently this year? What committees or other worship leadership will we need? It may be advisable to do some jotting down of plans even now on a month-by-month basis. Christmas, Easter, Young People's Day, and the like will come at their usual times. How shall we make the most profitable use of them? We may want to look ahead to several out-of-door services, and several symbolic rituals like the candle lighting service. This month-by-month planning may not be completed at this time, but it can be begun. In addition some attention may be given to the problem of church attendance on the part of youth.

d) *Outline roughly the fellowship program for the year.* Again some month-by-month planning is in order. We may want a New Year's party in January, and a mother-daughter banquet in May, and the like. We may also wish to fit in an evening or so with the entire church, and a joint evening of recreation with a youth group of another race or nationality. What committees or other organization will we need to make these a reality?

e) *Outline roughly the service program for the year.* What can we do to help our church during this coming year? We ought to plan at least one venture of this sort. What can we do for the relief of needy individuals? What can we do for the missionary cause? What can we do to combat social evil within our community or beyond? Or is there one outstanding social need into which we would like to sink all our efforts throughout the year? What organization will we need for this?

f) *Outline roughly other activities for the year.* Our emphases may commit us to some activities which do not fall neatly under any one of the four heads listed above. We may have decided, for example, to make more of dramatization than we have in the past. Or we may wish to put forth a special effort during the late spring to send a number of our young people to summer camp. All of these can stand some preliminary planning now, if time permits.

In some such way as this the responsible youth workers in a church may block out their inclusive program for a year. It should not be too rigidly fixed, but on the contrary extremely flexible and subject to change at many points as the twelve months unroll. When the day is done and the blueprint is finished, what then? Someone may be designated to report it in the "clearinghouse" of the congregation, where all the organizations of the church are represented and where it may be modified in the light of other plans. That would seem to be the honorable thing to do. Again, it may be reported to all the young people themselves in order that they may have a chance now—as they should have had before the retreat—to offer their suggestions freely. Finally, it must be put into effect. It is as yet only a blueprint. There is a long road with many a turning between the first blueprint and the finished structure. Many cabinet and committee meetings, keeping always a month or so ahead of the game, and much hard work will be necessary to turn it into a program which week by week will strengthen the Christian faith and life of the youth for whom it is intended.

A Typical Youth Plan Pictured

In the light of the foregoing we may now try our hand at picturing what a comprehensive plan of organization for youth work in a typical church might look like. What organizations will be required? What officers will they need? What committees? How will they be related to one another, and to the church as a whole? What will the entire plan look like? Questions such as these will not down.

In attempting to answer these questions we must think first of young people themselves and their spiritual growth. They are what counts—not organization. Organization is always a means to an end—never an end in itself. Organization is always slave—never master. Will youth live together more happily and share the Christian life more effectively in groupings of certain size and age range? Very well; we will organize accordingly. Do youth want to do certain things for themselves, the church, the community? Very well; we will have such officers and committees as are absolutely necessary—no more and no less. Do youth need the ever-present counsel of someone older than themselves? Very well; we will try to care for that through organization. Are the different youth groups sometimes prone to go their several ways forgetful of one another and of the rest of the church? Very well; we will try to remedy this defect through organization. And so at every point our plan of youth organization is secondary to youth themselves. It is merely our way of arranging things so that they can go forward in the Christian life together. It deserves to be called a good plan, not when it sounds impressive in a report or diagrams well on a blackboard; but when it helps young people to grow spiritually. Generally speaking, it should be as simple as possible; it should be quite easy to change; and it should shape itself by easy stages to fit a vital ongoing program—not the other way around.

Remembering these things, we may attempt to suggest a typical plan of organization for youth work. We have in mind a congregation of moderate size, with average leadership, and a building better than some and not so good as others. The principles we have been stating might work out somewhat as shown in the diagram on the opposite page.

THE CONGREGATION

CHILDREN OF THE CHURCH

Common Organization
Common Worship
Common Work
Common Play

YOUTH OF THE CHURCH

SENIORS–YOUNG PEOPLE (15-23)

1. Church School Department

MEETINGS
Sunday morning: for study principally
Sunday evening: worship, discussion of life problems
Occasional: fellowship, drama, activities of service

ORGANIZATION
Counselor   Teachers
Youth Officers
Committees: Program, Fellowship, Church Relations, Community Relations
Cabinet

2. Special Interest Groups
Choir, drama, missions, etc.

INTERMEDIATES (12-14)

1. Church School Department

MEETINGS
Sunday morning: study and worship (extended session, perhaps)
Weekday: chiefly class groups for fellowship and service

ORGANIZATION
Counselor   Teachers
Youth Officers
Committees: Program, Fellowship, Church Relations, Community Relations
Cabinet

2. Church Membership Class

3. Boy Scouts, etc.

ADULTS OF THE CHURCH

Including

Common Organization
Common Worship
Common Work
Common Play
Common Discussion

Class or Guild or League for Young Adults

A few comments may be in order, to clarify the suggestions embodied in the diagram.

It is obvious that the proposal of two church school departments—one for intermediates, and one for seniors and young people—is applicable only to churches of medium size. Smaller churches will not be able to have even two, and larger ones will have the full complement of three departments. In some congregations—probably a minority—it will not be feasible to make the church school the organizing center of youth work, as is here proposed.

This diagram aims to picture a plan of *organization* for youth work; it does not attempt to outline fully the *program* of youth work in a local church. Such a program comprises all the ways in which a congregation touches the lives of its youth, including notably the church service of worship. This program may be conveniently thought of and dealt with under the familiar fourfold division of study, worship, fellowship, and service. It would be seen as a whole and planned in its entirety at a beginning-of-the-year retreat such as was described in the preceding section, and then carried out through all the organizations and phases of the church's life which reach youth.

If the congregation is large and its youth work complex, there is need for something in the nature of a youth council representing all aspects of youth work and meeting periodically throughout the year to keep the youth program unified. This matter of unification is highly important. If it is not done well, some things will be done twice and others not at all—and youth will suffer.

The horizontal lines are "ties that bind" youth to the rest of the church. Theirs is the high purpose of keeping youth work an integral part of the congregation's life. They should prevent young people's organizations from becoming "free lances" or "lone eagles." These have been discussed in an earlier section of this chapter.

The youth officers referred to include the usual roster of president, vice-president, secretary, and treasurer. It may be useful to have a full and free discussion of the duties of these offices on occasion, especially before the time of election. The president presides at meetings of the department and of the cabinet with the adult counselor as his constant but not too obtrusive aid, appoints committees, visualizes plans and programs, and checks constantly to see that plans are being carried out according to schedule. (The younger and more immature the group, the more the adult counselor will have to take the reins; but he will relax his hold upon them as the officers grow in ability to carry responsibility, and he will work to that end.) The vice-president takes the place of the president in his absence, and in addition may assume some regular task such as the follow-up of absentees or the chairmanship of the program committee. In this way he grows in leadership capacity, and fits himself perchance to assume the presidency in his turn. The secretary keeps an accurate record of the meetings and activities of the group, attends to correspondence, and reminds the president of matters that require his attention. The treasurer keeps a careful account of all moneys received and expended, makes payments upon proper order, and presents vivid financial reports to the youth group so that they may be educated in Christian stewardship.

The committee plan given in the senior-young people column is not sacrosanct. It happens to be a setup which has been actually tried with success. The duties of the program and fellowship committees are self-evident. The church relations committee forms a bridge between the youth organization and the church as a whole. It fosters attendance at the church services, suggests projects of service to the local congregation as well as the denomination, and co-ordinates the youth program with any special emphases—such as international missions—which may be observed by the church from time to time. The community relations committee forms a similar bridge between the youth group and the surrounding community. It keeps tab upon Community Chest campaigns, housing conditions, relationships between racial and national groups within the community, and the like; and it proposes ways in which the department can take hold for the betterment of community life and the good of their own souls. The cabinet—or executive committee, as it may be called—co-ordinates the work of the several officers and committees, and promotes a unified youth program. The whole committee question will be given further consideration in a later chapter. One essential condition of good committee work may, however, be noted at this point—namely, that a competent adult be associated with each youth committee. This provision is especially necessary with intermediates.

Who, we may ask, is to take the lead in setting up and maintaining such an organizational plan as this? Again the answer must vary from congregation to congregation. In many instances it should be the minister himself. Certain ministers may even see their way clear to accept the counselorship of a church school department for youth. On the other hand, there are undoubtedly congregations where the initiative must be taken by a layman or laywoman—for example, a junior or senior high school teacher who gets along well with young people and is devoted to the Church. In all events, a youth plan such as we have been visualizing will most certainly fail without adequate adult guidance, and it deserves the best the congregation has to offer.

Such in brief is a skeleton outline of a youth plan for a typical congregation. The chapters which follow will attempt to fill in the outline in greater detail.

YOUTH AND THE CHURCH SERVICE

No CHURCH PROGRAM for youth is complete—whatever its other perfections—unless the young people attend the services of public worship regularly, intelligently, and gladly. If this is lacking, the congregation's own future is in peril and the young people themselves are being cheated spiritually. These are strong statements, but not too strong.

The truth of the matter is that a congregation can do something for its young people through the morning service that it can accomplish nowhere else. For here, if the conditions are right, youth can enter into the high experience of worship more fully than anywhere else. Here also they cultivate a sense of oneness with the fellowship of Christians—the local church, and the Church Universal both past and present. Here to a considerable extent their church membership becomes a living reality. Hence their regular and whole-souled participation in the church services is a major concern not only of the minister but of lay workers with youth as well.

There are quite a number of clear-thinking youth workers who hold sincerely that it is best not to expect younger intermediates and children to attend church every Sunday—an extended church school session with a rich and varied program is a desirable alternative—and that a few well-chosen

and well-planned experiences of worship with the entire
congregation each year may mean more to them than fifty-
two Sundays whose deeper meaning is beyond them. On
this point there is room for honest difference of opinion.
But all alike covet earnestly the presence of those fourteen
years of age and above—that is to say, from the time of full
church membership or enrollment in the church membership class.

As is so often the case in church work, however, what we
would like to see and what we actually see are not identical.
No doubt there are many congregations whose youth attend
as well as, or even better than, their elders. On the other
hand, in numerous churches youth are conspicuous largely
by their absence. One person curious on this subject asked
about three hundred ministers in three different cities how
many of them had trouble in getting young people to attend
the worship service of the church. All but twenty-three said
that they did.[1]

How, then, shall we get them to come? There are of
course innumerable devices which have been tried with more
or less success. Taking a record of church attendance in
much the same way as is commonly followed in church
school, giving credit or even awards for faithfulness, encouraging classes and other groups to attend in a body—all of
these have been put to the test. Sometimes as a last resort
young people are roundly scolded for their nonattendance.
At best these are only superficial tricks of the trade, and do
not get down to rock bottom. They merely endeavor to
make sure that youth will be there. They do not undertake
to insure that they will *want* to be there, or that they will
derive real spiritual benefit from being there. How can we
bring it about that they will want to be there?

YOUTH'S PART IN THE CHURCH SERVICE

There is a sound psychological principle to the effect that if you want to interest people in a program, you can do so by giving them a part in it. This principle is every whit as valid for the church service as for anything else, but extremely hard to apply in this particular case. For there are so few things that youth can do for and in the church service without violating long-established custom, or spoiling the service for other worshipers.

By and large the avenues of youth participation in the church service are three in number: first, *ushering;* second, *singing in the choir;* third, *conducting an occasional service.* Concerning the first of these little need be said. Young people may well do at least part of the ushering part of the time in the average congregation, and thus come to have a sense of ownership in its worship services. In some churches there is an ushers' league which makes of ushering almost a profession—giving careful attention to such matters as dress, the seating of visitors, and the reception of the offering, and working out a definite schedule in which every individual takes his turn.

As to the second of these, recent years have witnessed a startling rebirth of interest in chorus choirs as contrasted with mere paid quartets. This new development in the field of church music—it is almost a revolution—opens a promising way for large numbers of young people to participate most helpfully in congregational worship. A news item in a recent issue of a denominational journal reports nine-tenths of the youth group of a certain congregation attending church regularly, and the sponsorship by this group of a youth choir for the Sunday evening services.[2] One suspects that there is more than a casual connection between these two bits of news. As illustrative of what can be done through youth choirs, we may turn to the enthusiastic account which a minister of music has written of his own church's experience in this regard:

In our church the musical program is full-time work for one person. We have five organized choirs which rehearse every week. The Senior Choir, made up of young people of college age and over, sing at every morning service. Many of these young people would never attend church services otherwise. This choir has brought into the membership of the church a number of young married people who are seeking a place where they can be of service to it.

The Chapel Choir is a group made up of high school age young people who are given an opportunity to practice their Christianity. They sing every Sunday afternoon and find each other's company congenial. Parents have expressed gratitude that these young people are too busy in church to get into less desirable company elsewhere. For many of these young people the work in the choir is their social life as well. They are practically all members of the church and contribute regularly to its support.

The three Junior Choirs are composed of boys and girls from the age of seven to fifteen. They furnish the music for one afternoon service a month and are seen in regular attendance at church services. Their work in the choir has had the effect of bringing many of their parents into church membership in appreciation of the attractive program offered their children. In the past three years I can truthfully say that over two hundred persons have united with the church or the church school because of the musical program.

I feel that any church which would develop such a program would have no problem of attendance at church services on the part of its young people.

The values of such an extensive venture in sacred music are all too apparent. Fortunately, these values are not the monopoly of large congregations with full-time ministers of music. They can be realized within limits even in the humble church whose one and only choir warmly welcomes the talents of youth.

There remains the possibility of soliciting the interest of young people by inviting them to conduct or assist in conducting an occasional church service. This is more easily done in churches that have a free service than in those with the liturgical tradition. In either case it is probably wise to confine it, as a rule, to the evening service. Even this requires much careful guidance and coaching from start to finish on the part of the minister or some other person well trained in worship, if the venture is to leave a good taste in the mouths of all concerned.

One rural pastor experimented at some length and with real success in turning over some of his Sunday evening services to his young people. He describes the types of service which they presented. Some of their programs were constructed around hymns—hymns of the various denominations, hymns of different lands, old familiar hymns. Another type of service which met with favor recounted the experiences of the denominational camp in which some of the congregation's young people had shared. Still other services featured plays and pageants, drawn from such sources as *Twelve Months of Drama for the Average Church*.[3] On yet another occasion the church membership class presented a program on "How We Got Our Bible," which combined a period of worship, a dramatization, and a stereopticon lecture. The pastor is convinced that this series rendered a real service to the entire congregation, and at the same time helped materially to hold his young people to the church.[4]

WORSHIP—LITURGICAL AND OTHERWISE

Another sound approach to the problem of securing the attendance of youth at the church services is by way of making the worship as attractive to them as possible—attractive in the best sense of the word. (We are putting to one side for the moment the sermon, and thinking exclusively of the remainder of the service.) If they find it dull and uninspiring, or monotonously the same every Sunday, or shot through with concepts and language which they do not understand, of course they will not come and continue to come. How can we make our church services so attractive and meaningful and helpful to our young people that they will attend and participate gladly? And how can we do this without spoiling the service for the older folk, or departing too sharply from the traditions of the church and the accepted canons of good worship?

This leads inevitably to the question, How do youth feel about our present services? What do they themselves want in a service? What they want may not in every case be best or best for them, but their desires merit some consideration nevertheless. Unfortunately, we are largely in the dark concerning the answers to these simple questions. A feeble light at least is shed on the matter by a study which was made of the reactions of young people to two markedly different types of church service. Questionnaires were given to young people of congregations of the same denomination which worshiped almost across the street from one another but whose services were in the one case free and in the other liturgical. The groups were small, numbering about thirty each, and—as will be seen—not all of the young people answered every question. Their ages ranged from sixteen to twenty-five. They were without exception church members, and they had attended slightly more than half of the church services during the previous two months—the percentage being about the same in either instance. It may be helpful to examine their replies to some of the more significant questions:

Do you feel that you really worship God during the morning service?

Free church young people: Yes, 20; No, 4.

Liturgical church young people: Yes, 15; No, 0.

The difference here is not large, but it is clearly to the advantage of the liturgical church.

Can you recognize a certain progression in your own worship experience as the service moves along?

Free church young people: Yes, 6; No, 9.

Liturgical church young people: Yes, 11; No, 2.

Only one of the free church group revealed any real sense of progression from "creation of a worshipful attitude by the organ" at the beginning to "dismissal with a feeling that you have been closer to God." On the other hand, several of the other group were clearly aware of the psychological sequence within their own liturgical service. As one put it, "Forgiveness of our sins; praise to God; at the end a feeling of peace." Vogt and Sperry might do better, but this youth has a true sense of the development of his church's service. It should be pointed out that the sequence of the liturgical service is explained in the church membership class of this congregation.

Do you feel that you can worship better when the prayers are free or when they are read?

Free church young people: Free, 22; Read, 3.

Liturgical church young people: Free, 11; Read, 3; Both, 2.

This is one of the most unexpected responses in the whole questionnaire, particularly the replies of the youth from the liturgical church where prayers are read as a matter of course. One of this group says: "Often I think that prayers which are read do not always pertain to one's situation. They tend to become monotonous through repetition week after week."

Are there any portions of the service which make you feel very keenly the sense of God's presence? State them please. The young people from the free service mention music, prayers, and sermon most frequently. The young people from the liturgical church mention the confession and absolution, and the prayers chiefly. Four of this latter group indicate that intervals of silence, often with organ or chime music in the background, are especially conducive to the sense of God's presence. It is noteworthy that not one of the papers makes mention of the Scripture reading, unless "meditating upon the lesson" is so intended.

If you could make one change in the service of your church, what would it be?

    Free church young people: One wants the liturgical service; 7 desire more music by choir or organ; 1 less music; 3 shorter sermons.

    Liturgical church young people: 3 plead for more freedom and variety in the service.

These reactions provide much food for earnest thought. As one ponders them, certain conclusions stand out which may be taken as an extremely modest beginning toward a solution of the problem of youth and the church service.

1. *Youth respond rather favorably on the whole to a liturgy* —that is, a set form whose meaning and beauty can grow upon the worshiper through frequent repetition until it becomes a well-trod and beloved path between the soul and God. This should not appear strange to anyone who has witnessed the eager acceptance by young people of a candle-lighting ritual, for example. Not merely older persons but younger ones as well are altogether capable of appreciating beauty and orderliness in worship.

2. *Youth are very sensitive to needless monotony in a service, and resent it.* This fact stands out at more than one point in the foregoing questionnaire—particularly under the

question concerning free and read prayers. Perhaps it is that they are quick to memorize phrases and feel that they have drained all the sweetness out of them; then they are restless for a change. There can of course be change, and freshness, and prayers that fit a given moment—even within the framework of a liturgy. Probably a certain churchman is right in his oft-repeated statement that "the cure for liturgy is more liturgy."

3. *Youth are appreciative of periods of silence, particularly against the background of reverential music.*

4. *Youth get little from the Scripture lessons in the average service.* This is sad, but true. The reading of the Scripture, which should be God's word to man and hence of the utmost impressiveness, appears to register with them scarcely at all. Whether a wiser choice of lessons is needed, or a better reading of them, or a well-worded sentence of introduction and explanation, is difficult to say.

5. *Youth do not like sermons that are long, or seem to be long.* They probably feel the same way about the prayers of a service.

The study which has been cited, with the conclusions drawn therefrom, by no means covers the subject completely. Obviously it has to do principally with the form, not the content, of the service. A few of the additional points that have a claim to our consideration may be put in the form of questions.

6. *What kind of hymn means most to youth?* If young people were to choose the hymns for our church services, which ones would be sung most frequently? This is not to imply that young people should have the arbitrary power of sole choice by any means, but merely that their spiritual

hungers and aspirations are one of the factors to be considered in the selection of hymns for congregational singing.

7. *What sort of prayers would youth like to have offered on their behalf?* What concerns resting deeply upon their hearts would they like to see winged to the throne of grace through the medium of the minister's words?

8. *How do they react to the somewhat archaic language which is used in many of our services?* Do they appreciate its Shakespearean beauty, or does it at times mean little more to them than a foreign language would?

9. *Do they understand the theological concepts and phrases with which our worship abounds?* What, for example, does "the grace of God" mean to them? How far should we go in choosing words and forms that cannot possibly fail to be understood? Jesus used the simplest imaginable words and concepts, and the New Testament was written in the everyday speech of the period. Should we do likewise? It would seem possible to express sound religious thought in words of the day without falling at all into slang or ugliness of any sort. An alternative which commends itself to many is that we retain the time-honored and beautiful phrases of worship, and take pains to interpret them to our boys and girls so that their rich meaning will be apprehended.

This opens the way for one other matter which deserves to be considered under the head of youth and the church service—namely, *training youth for participation in worship.* Half of the battle for securing the hearty participation of boys and girls in a church service is won or lost long before the first strains of music open the service. It is won in the first place through an experience of true worship in both home and church school from childhood on. If young people have known a genuine approach to the Father of all life around the table and the family altar in their respective homes, and if the church school has week by week afforded them periods of true devotion, they are in so far forth ready and eager to enter into the worship of the congregation. It is won also through an earnest study of worship itself—what worship is, whom we worship, and what happens when we worship. Some of this study may well occur from time to time in church school classes or the young people's fellowship, and some of it—much of it—belongs also in the church membership class. And, finally, it is won through a painstaking analysis of the particular service in use in the church to which the young people belong. The order of the service can be examined—why this follows that, and how each part makes its own contribution to the finished service. Scarcely one boy or girl in ten will catch the beauty and the significance of this order without patient assistance. If this is done faithfully and well, we shall not have to worry quite so much about getting them to come to church.

PREACHING TO YOUNG PEOPLE

From one-third to one-half of the time of the typical Protestant church service is normally devoted to the sermon. It follows inevitably that the attractiveness of a church service to youth—still using the word in its best sense—will hinge to a considerable degree upon the sermon. We come, therefore, to another way of solving the problem of church attendance among young people—namely, to preach consciously to youth as well as to adults, to prepare the sermon and deliver it with them in mind.

But what is good preaching to young people? So far as *content* goes, we may unhesitatingly say it is preaching which brings the realities of our Christian faith to bear directly and helpfully upon the life problems and life needs of youth. On the one hand is the richness and fullness of our Christian heritage, its great doctrines concerning God and man and the world. On the other hand are the manifold things which youth are up against, some of which were surveyed in the first chapter of this book. Good preaching, in a word, throws light on the second of these out of the first. The sermonizer who is at home in both of these realms, and who can—to adopt another figure of speech—build a bridge of words across the gap which separates them so that spiritual help and strength can march out of our ancient Christian faith straight into the needy lives of youth today, will never want for an audience of young people.

So far as the *form* of good preaching to youth is concerned, that is a matter hard to get at. One way of getting at it is to examine sermons which have been actually preached to young people to see wherein their merit lies. Let us take, therefore, a book which was formed by securing from sixteen distinguished ministers of America their most representative messages to young people.[5] The sermons in this volume were in some cases, at least, delivered before students in educational institutions, and therefore depart somewhat from the preaching that the average minister does in the average church to a mixed congregation of youth and adults. Nevertheless, they may be presumed to be—and they are—good sermons, and they were designed especially for youth. It is interesting to analyze some of them for their form primarily, and endeavor to pry out the secret of their strength. Any such analysis is of necessity cold and mechanical, and perhaps incapable of catching what may be the true secret. Nevertheless, it may succeed in capturing a part of it.

Sermon No. 1

Seven illustrations. (It is difficult to say always just what is an illustration and what is not. Therefore another reviewer might have a different count in some instances.)

Clear fourfold structure.

Sermon No. 2

No illustrations, properly speaking.

Clear threefold structure.

Direct start; no fumbling about getting under way.

Many pungent, colloquial, semihumorous expressions: "Where have they been?" "They never got that idea from the Bible." ". . . . the sea where those other Israelites were splashing about."

The word "those" used seven times, as though the speaker had his audience with him in the scene he surveyed, and were pointing with his finger.

Sermon No. 4

Twelve illustrations.

Clear twofold structure.

A beginning which captures attention in the first sentence.

Some use of youth's language: "beautiful but dumb," "all hot and bothered."

Repetition with sledge-hammer effect of a single verse, "I bear them witness that they have a zeal for God, but not according to knowledge"—five times in two paragraphs.

Sermon No. 5

Six illustrations, in four of which young people figure.

No clear-cut divisions.

Has its origin in a distinct life situation of youth, namely, the drive for independence and self-expression following the first World War.

Sermon No. 6

Twelve illustrations.

Clear threefold structure.

The whole sermon is made to hang upon one word, the word "gentleman."

Considerable use of humor; half a dozen places where chuckles might be expected, but none toward the close.

Deals with a life problem of youth, What am I here for?

Sermon No. 7

No illustrations.

No clear-cut divisions.

Unexpected turn of thought—that is, the younger generation is accused of being too conservative.

Sermon No. 9

Three illustrations.

Clear fivefold structure.

Some telling sentences: "A tramp has been defined as a man who gained freedom but lost direction"; "I wouldn't soak my watch in hydrochloric acid. Why should I corrode my brain with alcohol?"

Sermon No. 14

Two full-fledged illustrations.

No clear-cut divisions.

Transparent honesty, no hedging or evasion—and on a difficult theological issue.

This analysis may offer us not so much the form of good preaching to youth, as the form of all good preaching. Perhaps these men would proceed in very much the same way, at least so far as form is concerned, if they were addressing a congregation of adults. Nevertheless, it is still true that these sermons represent the form and style which experienced preachers have found usable with youth. What, then, are the most obvious characteristics of good preaching as here revealed?

1. *A rather free use of illustrations.* The sermons average five each. Apparently the urgent need is felt for what someone has called "windows"—clear panes of glass through which the audience may peer into the truth which the preacher has in mind.

2. *A clear-cut structure,* easy to follow and easy to remember. In half of these cases the firstly, secondly, and thirdly are clearly discernible. In some the sermon is held together by what becomes almost a memory device—a word or a phrase upon which the whole discourse is strung.

3. *A speedy beginning,* which enlists interest and gets at the heart of the matter quickly without the tedium of a long-drawn-out introduction.

4. *Pungent phrases,* which rivet attention and stand to be remembered. In the sermons under consideration this characteristic at no point descends to the level of the cheap and the spectacular, but remains dignified and in good taste.

5. *A considerable understanding of what youth are thinking, what they are saying, and what they are worrying about.* One feels that these preachers are not talking to strangers, but to old acquaintances.

Here, then, is a beginning at least of the science of preaching and speaking to youth. Ministers and lay workers may test the truth of these principles, utilize them, and add to them as need arises and experience grows.

In conclusion, some mention should be made of the real value in an occasional thoroughgoing consultation between a minister and his young people concerning both the sermon and the order of service. Possibly few will find it feasible to go so far as did one minister who invited his youth to think through in class groups and society a series of topics upon which he was planning to preach. Two weeks before a given sermon a list of stimulating questions upon the proposed theme was submitted to church school classes of youth in mimeographed form. The classes discussed the questions with zest, and a careful record was preserved of their findings. The young people's society in turn continued the discussion, and a record was kept in similar manner. Finally the minister preached upon the much-discussed theme. The result was a heightened interest in both the sermons and the class and society sessions—in short, a clear gain all around.[6] There is no reason why such a plan could not be adopted occasionally in many churches—particularly when a special emphasis like missions or stewardship is before the congregation. But there are also lesser forms of co-operation between minister and youth which promise to be helpful to all concerned. The preacher can consult with his young people from time to time about the themes upon which they would like to have him preach. This is not to imply that they know more than he does concerning theology, or concerning the art of sermonizing; but they may know more than he does about their own problems, upon which they would like to receive help from him who is their spiritual guide. In the same manner, he may confer with them occasionally on the order of worship itself. Again, they are not liturgical experts; but they frequently have some decided ideas concerning what is appealing and helpful to them—and their ideas are not always bad ones. If their proposals are unworkable, the minister may unfold to them the good and sufficient reasons why the service is thus and so. If their requests are workable, the service is enriched and their own interest deepened. In either case they are given a glimpse into the inside workings of congregational worship, both service and sermon become more peculiarly their own, and a bond of fellowship is knit between a pastor and his young people.

We have approached this entire matter of youth and the church service with the primary question in mind, How can we get them to attend? This is a legitimate approach, but after all a rather superficial one. There is a question that goes far deeper—namely, How can we make our church services contribute genuinely to the spiritual upbuilding of our young people? In the final analysis it is to this end that we strive to find a place for them in the service, and that we try to fit both worship and sermon to their needs. If we care properly for the greater question, the lesser will tend to care for itself.

V

YOUTH AND THE CHURCH SCHOOL

A GOOD CASE CAN be made for the position that we should first exhaust the possibilities of youth work in the church school before allowing ourselves to set up other youth groups and organizations. To lay this down as an infallible rule for every church would, of course, be a fatal mistake. On the other hand, some persuasive reasons come to the support of this position in many instances.

1. *In the average church we already have a larger percentage of the available young people enrolled in the church school than we are likely to reach through any other program.*

2. *The part of wisdom in church work is to have as few organizations as possible, and to set up no new agencies until the possibilities of existing ones have been squeezed dry.*

3. *The church school still has the hours during which people in most communities are least likely to be occupied with other things.*

These are some of the very practical and homely reasons why in many churches, at least, it seems wise to make the most of the church school, and then—if need be—supplement it with other ventures in youth work.

There are churches, particularly in the country, so genuinely handicapped by lack of space that it is next to impossible to do good work with youth in the church school. In some of them there can be no separate youth department, and that is all there is to it. There is no room. Many of them cannot even provide a modicum of quiet for church school classes, but must ask them to meet alongside of other classes—all going full tilt at the same time. And yet it is safe to say that countless churches could make more room for youth in the church school than they are now doing. Sometimes it is a matter of asking adult classes, whose numbers have shrunk but whose quarters have not, to share their space with younger groups. Sometimes it is a matter of fewer and larger classes throughout the school, thus opening the way for a better use of the facilities at hand. Sometimes it is a matter of renovating or rebuilding—from partitioning a balcony or excavating a basement to the erection of a new structure. Sometimes a near-by house can be claimed for certain of the classes and departments, thus freeing more space for others. Sometimes the only way out seems to be the use of the church sanctuary for church school purposes. There are many people who object quite honestly to such an expedient. Their objections might not be pressed so hard if they could be sure that the sessions held in the sanctuary would be conducted in decency and good order.

A certain church school found itself at one stage in its history meeting in three overly large departmental groups. One of these comprised fifteen classes, trying valiantly but vainly to study in a single unpartitioned room. The young people had no separate room, no separate department, no place of their own. Meanwhile a church sanctuary with a seating capacity of twelve hundred went entirely unused during the church school hour. After a thorough canvass of the situation it was decided to utilize the sanctuary and to

reallot some of the remaining space within the church building. The net result was the division of the school into five
departments instead of three, one of the new departments
being a youth group. This was accomplished without ex-
pending a cent of money, or doing injury to any part of the
building. Where there is a will, there is very often a way.

The Setup of a Youth Department

Wherever circumstances permit it, a youth department—
or departments—is the ideal which insistently beckons to us
in church school work with youth. We turn our attention
now to some of the details of such a department.

A separate *meeting place* is almost a necessity, but not
quite so. It is not too hard to imagine such a department
compelled to share a room on Sunday morning with other
classes, and yet having its own organization and its own life—
chiefly in weekday or weeknight meetings for planning, for
social fellowship, and the like. Far better, however, is a
series of adequate classrooms, plus a chapel or assembly
room suitable for true worship. The "worship center" may
be an altar with cross and candles, or it may be a fireplace
surmounted by a picture of high religious quality and flanked
by chairs in semicircular rows and a floor lamp or so. This
last named arrangement lends itself excellently to worship,
discussion, and informal fellowship—all three.

A workable *form of organization* for a youth department
includes first of all the usual set of officers, elected entirely
by the young people themselves without any interference
from the rest of the school. In addition there is required
an adult counselor chosen by the school in whatever manner
the general officers are elected—preferably in this case after
some consultation with the young people themselves to make

sure that the person chosen will be one whom they can accept without reserve. Besides these, there may be the necessary standing committees. The officers, the counselor, the committee chairmen, and perhaps the teachers—if this does not make too many adults—together constitute a cabinet whose monthly meetings are the living heart of the department.

An impressive practice both in local youth groups and in youth camps is to set apart those who are charged with special responsibilities in *a service of installation*. The suggestions which follow draw upon the work which others have done in the preparation of such services. They constitute a very simple ritual, which should for best effect be carried through slowly and reverently.

On the altar or table is a candlestick with a large lighted candle, or else a candelabrum containing several candles. The departmental counselor takes his place before the altar. All the members of the department are supplied with small candles.

COUNSELOR: All we who bear the name of Christian and stand within the Christian fellowship look to Jesus of Nazareth as the author and finisher of our faith. He is the radiant source alike of the ideals which lure us on in all we undertake, and of the faith which sustains us in all we undergo. He is "the true Light which lighteth every man that cometh into the world." "In him was life; and the life was the light of men." As I assume the responsibilities of my office I take a flame for my candle from the central light of all, in humble acknowledgment of the fact that my own life needs to be illumined from him who is the light of the world.

(Counselor lights his candle.)

COUNSELOR: Will the officers of the department, the chairmen of committees, and the teachers step forward. . . . . You have been chosen to lead the way in the work of our department— our worship, our study, our fellowship, our service to mankind.

Your tasks will not be easy ones. Do you now pledge yourselves to the fullest service which you can render?

RESPONSE: We do, trusting in that help which comes from above.

COUNSELOR: Take, then, light for your candles. "Let your light so shine before men that they may see your good works, and glorify your Father which is in heaven."

(Those named light their candles from the candle of the Counselor.)

COUNSELOR (addressing the department): The success or failure of our life together depends not alone upon us who stand before you. Each of you bears his own share of responsibility. Do you now pledge yourselves, each one, to the fullest co-operation which you can render?

RESPONSE: We do, trusting in that help which comes from above.

COUNSELOR: Take, then, light for your candles. "Let your light so shine before men that they may see your good works, and glorify your Father which is in heaven."

(Officers, chairmen, and teachers turn and light the candles of those in the front row of the department; they in turn light the candles of those in the second row; and so on till all are lighted.)

COUNSELOR: Let us pray. Almighty Father, bless the words of our lips and the intentions of our hearts this hour. In the months which lie ahead keep us ever faithful to the vows which we have professed before thee and before one another. We know how much of darkness there is within each one of us. May something of the radiance which was in Jesus Christ shine into our souls, and through us into our world, until in thine own good time the blackness of sin and suffering shall disappear, and the whole earth shall be bright with thy glory. Through Jesus Christ, our Lord. Amen.

SINGING BY ALL: "Follow the Gleam."

There remains the troublesome issue of *proper grading*, which comes down chiefly to the question of what ages can

live and study and work together well. In a very large
school with numbers enough and room enough for many
classes and several youth departments, this is no problem
at all. But smaller and average-sized churches must of necessity make age combinations. What combinations are best?
A great deal of thinking and practical experience underlie a
set of proposals for grouping put forward recently by a competent worker with youth. For a large church he recommends the following groups: seventh grade, eighth and ninth
grades, tenth to twelfth grades, college youth, those employed but unmarried, and young married couples. For a
church of medium size the recommendations run as follows:
seventh and eighth grades, ninth to twelfth grades, young
people beyond high school but unmarried, and young married couples. For a small church it is suggested that the
seventh grade be placed with the younger children, grades
eight to twelve be put together in one group, and all those
above high school age be constituted a second group.[1] These
groupings do not coincide precisely with those commonly
made in either church school or public school; they are worth
studying nevertheless.

Closely related problems—still in this matter of grouping—
are whether boys and girls should be together in the same
class, and how large the classes should be. As to the former
question, there is probably more to be said for putting the
sexes together than for segregating them. They are together in public school; why not in church school? There
might be fewer marital squabbles and less business for the
divorce courts if boys and girls had abundant opportunity
to get one another's viewpoint during the period of adolescence. Besides, in the medium-sized school the problem of
grouping is cut in half if coeducation is the rule rather than

segregation. As to the latter question, the trend in Christian education is rather clearly toward somewhat larger classes than has frequently been the case in our church schools. One of the chief reasons for this trend is the greater ease of finding a competent teacher for each class if the classes are not quite so numerous. And a group of twenty under a good teacher seems preferable to a group of ten under a poor teacher. This may seem to be rather hard and cold logic, but it is not bad logic at all.

The Curriculum

The word "curriculum" is being used here primarily in the sense of study curriculum. This is not to deny for a moment the importance of other phases of the program, but merely to concentrate attention on what is perhaps the chief function of the church school—namely, study. What shall be the curriculum of study in the youth classes of the church school? By and large, there are two main answers to this question.

One is that the several classes will follow *a lesson series,* commonly that of the denomination to which the school belongs. The various denominations provide well-designed courses of lessons—generally one for intermediates (twelve to fourteen), one for seniors (fifteen to seventeen), and one for young people (eighteen to twenty-three). In addition, there is available an excellent series with no denominational coloring which offers a separate course for each year from twelve to seventeen inclusive.[2]

To follow a lesson series is the easiest possible way out of the curriculum difficulty, and probably in many cases the best. It does, however, bring with it the serious problem of *motivation*—that is, how can we whip up sufficient interest in courses that come along as regularly as the seasons, and just as independently of the wishes of youth? "So what?" comes all too close to being the reaction, spoken or unexpressed, of many a youth when the spick-and-span quarterlies are distributed for the first time. If this indifference is to be overcome, heroic measures are needed. A carefully planned campaign is required, as detailed as any general ever laid out before an approaching battle. If all the teachers who are using a given quarterly will meet before each new quarter, they can plan a campaign of interest capturing. First of all, they themselves can become enthusiastic over the new area of study and its manifold possibilities. Then they can discuss ways and means of using that first Sunday for introducing class and quarterly to each other in a warm and hearty manner. They can help the class to see the quarter's work as a whole. They can throw out questions which whet interest. They can give true-false tests on the subject matter to be covered. They can show how the new area will gear helpfully into the lives of the young people. They can dangle before their eyes the interesting things to be done during the weeks ahead. "Well begun, half done" is perhaps the supreme rule for insuring profitable use of a lesson series.

Inasmuch as many of our church school classes will probably find themselves using a given lesson series for some time to come, let us go a little deeper into the question of how to make best use of a lesson quarterly. Suppose, for example, that next Sunday's lesson has to do with the Macedonian call and Paul's earliest experiences on the continent of Europe (Acts 16). The class is a group of high school youth—boys and girls. It is Monday or Tuesday evening— not Saturday—and the teacher sits down with quarterly before him. What does he do first? And then what? Conceivably he might spend a good hour or more as follows:

1. *What is this lesson about?* Not a careful study as yet—merely a quick survey.
2. *What do my pupils need most within the field of this lesson?* After serious consideration one of these two may be decided upon:
   - *a)* An accurate knowledge of some facts of Paul's missionary career.
   - *b)* Stimulation of interest in the present-day missionary enterprise.
3. *What experiences can I provide to take my class toward this objective?* A number of ways of spending the half-hour suggest themselves, from which two or three must be chosen:
   - *a)* A vivid telling on my part of the story of Paul's crossing into Europe.
   - *b)* Joint study of the quarterly and the Bible to get this story.
   - *c)* The use of maps and pictures.
   - *d)* The reading of the travel-diary of a modern missionary.
   - *e)* An earnest discussion of the case for missions today.
   - *f)* A visit to the class by a real flesh-and-blood missionary.
4. *What help does the quarterly have to give on the foregoing question?* Now is the time for a careful study of both pupil's and teacher's quarterlies.
5. *Sketching on paper a lesson plan for next Sunday.*

Great spiritual benefit can come from the consistent use of a good lesson series—of this there can be no doubt! The secret lies largely in putting the young people first, and the quarterly second. We do not teach a quarterly; we teach people with the aid of a quarterly.

An unsolved problem as yet in many church schools is how to get the quarterlies read and used—not the teacher's quarterly as a rule, but the pupils'. Some of them are taken home and forgotten; many of them are "as good as new" when the quarter ends; a few of them are read and used. If all the money virtually wasted on pupils' quarterlies were added together, it would surely pay some war debt or other. A promising solution to this problem, which deserves richly to be tried out in many classes, involves a good, long class session with part of this time devoted then and there to the reading of the lesson materials under the constant guidance and inspiration of the teacher. It is nothing more nor less than a plan of guided study, which has proved so successful in public school and may be equally rewarding in the church school.

The other answer to the curriculum question is *the elective system*—each class choosing its own course of study from time to time in accordance with its own peculiar interests and needs. This answer tends to care very well for the problem of motivation, but raises in turn another equally difficult—namely, the problem of *balance*. For the elective system leads quite easily to a lopsided spiritual diet. A class pursuing this plan may find itself devoting all of its time to social issues and none to the content of the Bible, or the other way around. In order to escape this pitfall, the teachers of youth classes—or better still the teachers and youth representatives in joint conference—may construct a list of required and elective courses exactly as is done in most colleges and high schools. The required courses would represent those areas of study to which it is felt all youth of a given age should get around sooner or later. The elective courses would allow a measurable freedom of choice above and beyond the essential curriculum. In no case would any unit of study have to be taken at any set time.

As an illustration of how such a plan might work out, the following list is suggested.[3] It will be noticed that the number of required units decreases and the number of elective units increases as the young people grow more mature. Because of their crucial importance, a course in the life of Jesus and a survey course in the Bible are included under each age. A good deal is made of biography with the inter-mediates because of the special flair which they seem to have for heroes and hero worship. No specific treatment of church membership is provided for this age in the church school; this is left rather to the church membership class. Vocational guidance is placed in the senior age, because it is at that period of life that serious thought must be given to the choice of a life work. Other instances of the appropriateness of a unit of study to a given age will be apparent. With these preliminary explanations let us look at a tentative plan for securing proper balance under the elective system.

REQUIRED AND ELECTIVE COURSES FOR CHURCH SCHOOL YOUTH

Intermediate or Junior High School (12-14)—12 three-month units

REQUIRED	ELECTIVE
The life of Jesus	The story of Christian hymns
Great leaders of the Church	Getting along at home
How we got our Bible	Getting along at school and play
How to pray	
What makes a thing right or wrong	Our bodies and how they grow
Great missionaries of the Church	Our wonderful world of nature
	Old Testament heroes
The stories of the prophets	
Christian neighborliness to those in need (study plus action)	

Senior or Senior High School (15-17)—12 three-month units

REQUIRED	ELECTIVE
Choosing a life work	Alcohol—what it does to the individual and society
Boy-girl relationships	
The story of our Bible	The drama of Christian missions
Understanding ourselves	
The history of the Christian church	God in nature
The life of Jesus	The Christian and other races
	Youth and their parents
	Christian art and artists
	The Christian and community problems (study plus action)
	The life of Paul
	The life and work of Isaiah (or Jeremiah)
	Some good uses of leisure time

Young People (18-23, in college or employed)—24 three-month units

REQUIRED	ELECTIVE
Preparation for Christian home life	Youth work in the church
A Christian's citizenship	How to teach in the church school
The content of our Bible (2 units)	Organizing the church for Christian education
The life of Jesus	Science and religion
War and peace	How to be a Christian though employed
Christianity and economics	How to be a Christian though unemployed
The Church at work in the world—past and present	Religion and the fine arts
	Helping other young people to be Christian
	The task of missions today
	Intensive study of individual books of the Bible

Drama in the church

The devotional life of a Christian

A Christian view of history

The movement for union among the churches

The worship of our church and others

The religion of the Hebrews

Ventures in understanding other races and groups

Social assets and liabilities of our community (including action)

The history of our denomination

What is Christian social action?

The elective system raises other problems besides that of securing proper balance in the curriculum. The one of the expense of the study books required seems insoluble at first, but is not in reality. The outlay during the first year may frighten the budget-makers, but if the books purchased are retained by the school and used time after time the average expense over a period of years is not prohibitive by any means. A more pressing problem is, Where can suitable study materials be found? The worker perplexed by this question has at least four sources to which he can turn. In the first place, individual units can often be lifted out of a conventional lesson series and used according to the elective plan. In the second place, the major denominations publish catalogues of elective courses which can be had for the asking. In the third place, the well-known pamphlets of the United Christian Youth Movement [4] contain in each case extensive bibliographies of materials suitable for use in young people's classes. In the fourth place, the bulletin *Learning for Life*[5] is an invaluable classified, annotated list of study materials designed originally for adults but usable also in many instances with young people.

All in all, the elective system is not an easy way, but it is probably the best way in all youth classes which are ready for it. In all likelihood the day will come when most of our church schools will adopt it in their work with youth. When that day arrives, there may be no such hard-and-fast division into classes as we now know, but young people will group and regroup themselves according to the subjects they wish to study. And, when that day arrives, we may hope that young people will throw themselves into their study of the Christian faith and life with a new zest and a new diligence.

YOUTH IN THE SMALL CHURCH SCHOOL

The complaint is sometimes heard that many of the suggestions for youth work seem to proceed on the assumption that the average church school has a membership of a thousand, a plant covering the better part of a city block, and a location next door to a library, an art gallery, and a college. In actual fact, the typical school throughout our nation—particularly in the open country—does not quite fit this description. In 1930 the average rural church school had an enrollment of only sixty-six, and two-thirds of such schools met in one or two rooms.[6] What, we may well stop to ask, can be done for youth in the small church school—small in numbers and small in building?

To begin with, as has already been intimated, it may be possible to have an organized youth department even though no separate meeting place is available on Sunday morning.

If there are as many as two or three classes within the age range of fifteen to twenty-three, they can be banded together in a department whose distinctive activities are scheduled for weekdays, weeknights, and Sunday evening. This is scarcely a perfect arrangement, but much of the best church work has been done under conditions that were far from perfect.

Where even this is not feasible, we fall back necessarily upon *the class* as the center of youth work in the church school. The organized church school class has on the whole a somewhat spotty record. It has done much good, and also some harm. At times it has been not merely organized but overorganized, with such a wealth of pins, mottoes, banners, officers, and activities that the class members could see nothing but their own class. The church as a whole was scarcely visible through the haze of class paraphernalia. But in the small church school, where a more inclusive youth organization is out of the question, the organized class has a rightful place. It can have its officers and committees without any compunctions of conscience, chosen yearly or perhaps twice a year in order to share the responsibilities among a larger number. It can have a well-rounded program including not merely study, but also worship, fellowship, and service. It may even have a motto and a class pin, provided the members are on their guard against a too narrow class loyalty. This danger can safely be averted if the class will meet with others in the church from time to time, work with others, and think of themselves constantly as being a true part of their church.

Beyond all this, the young people in the small church school can be given a share in the worship of the school. If they cannot have separate services of their own, they can at least take the responsibility for the worship in the "main department" once a month and thus enlarge their place in the school's life.

We have spoken thus far as though the lot of the small church school were all liabilities and no assets. Nothing could be farther from the truth! The small church does have liabilities—there is no use blinking that fact. Its building is often small; its musical instruments poor; its appointments bare and unlovely; its supply of maps, pictures, and books practically nonexistent. But it also has assets, points of strength which go with its very smallness and help rather than hinder its work with youth.

Foremost among these is a fact of immeasurable importance which has not had the attention which is its due—namely, that the small church can more readily than its larger neighbor become a closely knit fellowship with a strong influence upon each young life within the fellowship. For each church is a social group with folkways of its own—ways of thinking and acting which belong to it and constitute its character and personality. In so far as these ways of thought and life derive from the person of Jesus of Nazareth, each congregation may be regarded as a carrier of the Christian heritage. And these folkways it tends constantly to imprint upon every growing life in its midst—not so much by what it says to them as by what it is before them. Only—and this is the point which concerns us—it does so in exact proportion to the compactness of its fellowship. If the members of the church know one another well, if they see one another often during the week, if they are friends and neighbors to one another, the ways of the group will influence strongly the ways of each individual; otherwise not. In a small congregation the conditions for this flow of group ideals into individual lives are met almost automatically.

Let the worker in the small church school, therefore, thank God and take courage. His church, with its intimate fellowship, its cheery greetings, its friendly gossip, its Fourth of July picnics, and its Christmas exercises, has ways of reaching youth which are as vital and life-giving as anything the latest standard can measure or the latest book recommend. A congregation, of course, cannot send down through these channels what it does not possess. But whatever it has of Christian faith and idealism will go down into the next generation with scarcely an effort. We need not even bother greatly to see to it that this happens; the Almighty saw to it long ago.

In addition to this asset of a compact fellowship which is the rightful possession of all small churches alike, there is a spiritual advantage which belongs peculiarly to the country church by virtue of the fact that it is set in the very midst of God's handiwork instead of man's. Life in the country does seem conducive to a "closer walk with God."

One of the secrets not only of the popularity but also of the spiritual effectiveness of the religious summer camp has been the fact that it brings youth—many of whom are city-dwellers—face to face with nature. The morning watch by stream or lake, the evening services from vesper hill—these derive a large part of their religious suggestiveness from their natural setting. But these same spiritual resources which the summer camp must labor so hard to command are at the constant disposal of the humblest country church. The rural church school may not have a rich library of books for leading men to God, but it has some of His own volumes. It ought to turn the pages of these volumes frequently, and interpret them to God's children.

What, then, shall we say of the small church school and its youth? Has it a chance with them? Perhaps, when all is said and done, it has every whit as good a chance as the larger school. It can never hope for elaborate equipment. It ought not to try to duplicate the forms of organization which work splendidly in congregations of a thousand members. But there is nothing to prevent it from having quiet and reverential worship, or vital study under devout teachers, or actual work for the kingdom of heaven. And all that it does can be enveloped in what it is—a closely knit Christian fellowship. The small church school can meet all the essential conditions for growth in Christian character, and meet them well.

There is a verse in the New Testament which reads: "Fear not, little flock; for it is your Father's good pleasure to give you the kingdom." One is sometimes tempted to wonder whether the word "little" really belongs in this verse. Perhaps it is not a mistake after all.

THE YOUTH SOCIETY OR FELLOWSHIP

ON A WINTER'S DAY in the year 1881 the Christian Endeavor Society was founded by—as almost everyone knows—Francis E. Clark in Portland, Maine. From that day to this the young people's society has occupied a leading place in the youth work of American Protestant churches. The Christian Endeavor Society itself grew by leaps and bounds, while the denominations one by one developed their own organizations—Leagues and Unions which reached down into local churches and produced countless Sunday evening meetings for young people in city and country from coast to coast. The fortunes of the years have been kindly on the whole to this gigantic movement. In spite of a few setbacks it has branched out in new directions in recent times, and still challenges vigorously the attention of all who concern themselves with youth work in the church. The youth society or fellowship is a "live option" for any church, and for every youth worker.

SHALL WE HAVE ONE?

This question may sound a bit impertinent, but it is not meant to be so. After all, no agency or organization has any inherent right to a place in your church and mine. It should be made to prove its title to such a place, and prove it clearly. There are many churches which need a youth society or fellowship desperately, and there are others where it would be a mistake to set one up. It is therefore quite in order to ask, Shall we have a youth society or fellowship in our church? And, as is so often the case, our answer to this question depends upon the replies which we first give to certain other questions.

Is there space in our church building for a youth department in the church school?

Would a youth department in the church school have freedom to be of, by, and for youth?

Does the denominational program take the form principally of a League or Union or Fellowship which recommends Sunday evening meetings for local groups?

What has been most successful in our church in years past?

Is the need felt for more time than the church school affords?

Finally, when is the time of our young people most free from conflicting interests and engagements? Is it Sunday morning? Or is it Sunday evening? Or is it a weeknight?

Upon all these considerations hinges our answer to the question, Shall we have a youth society or fellowship?

WHO SHALL BE IN IT?

This raises once again the persistent problem of grading—what ages can work together profitably and harmoniously? Generally speaking, the youth society has not been as careful in this matter as the church school, and not always as careful as it might have been.

As a first step toward answering this question, can we say that there is little use by and large in trying to combine younger intermediates—twelve and thirteen—with high school and older youth in a single society? There may be small churches where all these diverse ages will be happy together, but in most churches it cannot be done successfully, and there is little point in trying it. Either the intermediates will not come despite all our pleadings and inducements, or—if they come—they will tend to be disinterested spectators in the discussions and troublesome wallflowers in the social activities.

As a second step, can we say truthfully that by and large those twenty-five years of age and over should not remain any longer in a young people's society? A couple of them may continue as counselors with benefit to both themselves and the group as a whole, but most of them should be given some other niche in the church's fellowship. Here we put our finger upon a sore spot in more than one youth organization. Young people grow up in the society. It has meant and still means a great deal to them. But now Father Time has completed a part of his task, and they are older. If they continue to cling to the beloved organization, they are likely because of their greater maturity and experience to hold too many offices and speak too often in the discussion—with the result that the 'teen-age youth drop more and more into the background, and finally fall away altogether. The obituary notice of more than one society or fellowship, we fear, could be written in the words of this last sentence.

It would be a cruel injustice to scold the older youth—or younger adults—for the existence of this situation. It is not their fault. The truth is that frequently they have no other place to go. There literally is no place in the church organization where they can feel perfectly at home. We shall come back in a later chapter to this phase of the problem. For the moment we may say simply that the best solution lies in providing other outlets for the young adults and for the still older people who may be in the habit of attending. Yet another is to talk the matter out frankly and lovingly, with the possible result of making some other provision for those around twenty-five and over.

We have thus by a process of elimination narrowed down the workable age range for a society or fellowship to *about the years fifteen to twenty-three inclusive*. It is hard to see how this can be stretched far one way or the other without defeating the very purposes for which such an organization exists. For those above and those below, other places in the life of the church can be found to the mutual advantage of all concerned. In large churches even this nine-year span may be subdivided, and covered by two or three groupings instead of one.

How Shall It Be Organized?

The answer to this question can be briefly given by repeating almost verbatim what was said under this heading in the case of the church school youth department; namely, the usual officers, plus an adult counselor, plus committees— all of these (committee chairmen only, not committee members) constituting a cabinet with regular monthly meetings. Of the three items in this setup the middle one, the adult counselor, for some strange reason is the one most likely to be overlooked. To cut a society adrift without any adult help is every bit as bad as loading it down with the presence of too many adults. Either extreme may prove fatal.

A word deserves to be said about the matter of *committees*. Two schemes for getting the most out of committees have been proposed and used in youth groups. The older one is the large committee or commission plan. The crux of this scheme lies in dividing the entire membership into three or four large committees—program, fellowship, and the like—thus making sure that every person will serve on a committee. A recent development, and perhaps a more promising one, makes much use of short-term committees which have a specific task to do, do it, and are discharged. To illustrate, a standing committee or the cabinet as a whole may block out the recreational program for the entire year, but a short-lived committee will be made responsible for a Valentine Party, another for a Mother-Daughter Banquet, and so on through the year. This plan may turn out to be the best yet devised for making something of committees. There is a real appeal in tackling a definite job, carrying it out to a successful conclusion, and then knowing that you are through. This plan also lends itself nicely to the project or activity or interest-group programs which so many fellowships are adopting nowadays. A group engaged in a project of fellowship with Negroes, for example, will find a place for a short-term committee to plan a worship service, and another to arrange a visit to a Negro church, and another to prepare a chart on white and Negro schools; and all of these will have a vitality about them which standing committees find it hard to match.

A word deserves to be said also about the fairly common practice of appointing each society member in turn as *the leader of the meeting.* At the risk of sounding undemocratic, it may be doubted whether this is the wisest practice. In the average youth fellowship there are few young people, perhaps none, who are truly qualified to lead a discussion helpfully; and not all by any means are fitted as yet to take a major share in the conduct of worship. Would it not be better to reserve such difficult tasks for the adult counselor and a limited number of the more competent young people? The others can get real satisfaction and at the same time grow into capable leadership through playing lesser roles in the society's life—and the program itself will not suffer.

Finally, some note should be taken of the fact that the trend in youth work is unmistakably toward less and less organization. There was a time when the organization was set up first, and then tasks were found for the organization to do. More recently it is often the other way around: first a live fellowship of young people evolves some purposes which it would like to achieve, with merely a hint of an officer or so to carry it through this stage; then it sets up a fluid organization as needed to achieve these purposes. Such an organizational scheme may change from year to year or even from month to month, and it may look slightly hit-or-miss when diagramed on a piece of paper, but it works in both senses of the word—it works out well, and it gets work done.

One convenient way for cutting organization to the bone is to make the same set of officers do double duty for both the morning church school session and the evening society meetings, where both exist. An actual account of how such a plan operates may well bring to a close this part of our discussion.

The Young People of ——— is an amalgamation of the senior-young people's department of the church school which meets on Sunday morning, and the league which meets in the evening. Any member of either group is considered a member of the whole, though, as is the case in morning and evening church services, some have a preference for one or the other and attend that one almost exclusively.

The officers are those of the regular league setup; namely,

president, four vice-presidents, secretaries, treasurer, editor of
"The Loudspeaker" (a weekly), pianists, etc. They are elected
annually by both groups. The president heads up the whole,
and reports to the pastor on equal footing with the church school
general superintendent. The morning session is governed by the
senior-young people's counselor, who is elected annually by the
church school board and reports to this board. However, he
works closely with the president of the young people, and is
also a member of the young people's cabinet.

Offerings in the morning go to the church school treasury,
those in the evening to the young people's treasury. The membership is about 225, with an average attendance in the morning
of about 120, and in the evening of about 90.

What Shall Be Its Program?

It is doubtful whether any other branch of church work
has witnessed as striking a variety in type of program as the
youth society or fellowship. Each separate one is likely to
obey the biblical injunction of doing what seems right in its
own eyes. There is something hopeful in this variety. It
at least means that many youth fellowships are giving play to
their own ingenuity and their own sense of need in program
construction. On the other hand, the results may not be in
every case educationally sound, nor spiritually most helpful.

Let us call the roll, as it were, of a number of types of
program one by one, without trying especially to label them
as either good or bad.

1. Many young people's societies *follow a prescribed series
of topics* week by week without change. This is of course
by all odds the easiest way to arrive at a program, but it is
not necessarily the best—except in the case of newly organized groups and very young groups with a shortage of capable older advisors. The society that desires to follow
this procedure is not left without an abundance of materials

from which to choose. The Christian Endeavor topics have a long and honorable history, and are continually under going change and improvement. One denomination—there may be others—publishes a regular quarterly for youth societies.[1] Many denominations provide a constant flow of well-chosen and well-prepared study units in their youth periodicals.

For many groups—particularly those that are rather young, or those whose leadership is rather new at the business of program building—the wisest plan for the present at least may be simply to follow a given series of topics week by week without change. And there is no doubt in the world that much good can be derived from such a program, provided the topics are used in the right way. Let us suppose that the topic prescribed for a Sunday evening several weeks in the future is "Youthful Criminals in America." The hour can of course be spent by having several persons stumble through the reading of a few clippings from the pages of the denominational youth paper—but the average society will not survive many such evenings. Instead we picture a small committee sitting down in advance with their adult counselor, youth periodical in hand, to lay their plans. What specific corner of this topic will interest our group most— how many young criminals there are in America, how many in our own community, what makes them criminals, what becomes of them afterwards, or what we can do about it? This is the first question. The second follows closely. How can we handle this topic in the most interesting and helpful way—a talk by a local judge or probation officer, a chart making statistics come alive, a panel discussion on why young people go wrong, a free-for-all discussion on what we can do about it, or several reports by our own members based on the materials in the youth paper? It is precisely to answer this question that the materials in the youth periodical were written. So now the committee members search these pages with a fine-tooth comb. Finally a plan for this Sunday evening begins to stand out. It is their own plan. It fits their own group. It is somewhat different from the plan a society ten miles away will decide upon. And yet it may have in it much of the material and many of the suggestions which were found in the pages of the youth periodical.

2. A worth-while step up the ladder in program building is to *examine in advance the topics in a given series, choose only those of genuine interest, and fill in the gaps with topics and activities which the group itself selects.* This is a step upward which can conscientiously be recommended to many societies which have thus far contented themselves with a wholesale adoption of some series or other. The question will at once arise, Where shall we find materials for filling in the gaps? For this business of gap-filling, as well as for the construction of one's own program from scratch, there is scarcely anything better than the undated units of the Epworth League. These units are inexpensive. They are well-written. They cover almost every possible area into which young people will want to enter. They are largely undenominational in character. Each of them contains enough material for three to five weeks as a rule. And they are arranged on three levels of difficulty—for intermediates, seniors, and young people. No group need feel lost for resource-materials if it has on its shelves a number of these units.[2] Valuable undated program units are published by other denominational houses as well, notably the Pilgrim Press.[3]

3. A very elementary but workable way of taking hold of

a program is to *note first the special days which may be help-fully observed in a given quarter, and then fill in the gaps with topics and activities which the group desires.* For example, a committee of a certain youth fellowship sat down to survey the January-March quarter and lay their plans for that period. When the special days ahead were noted, the calendar began to shape up in this fashion:

> January   4—New Year's Service
>   11—
>   18—
>   25—
> February   1—
>   8—Foreign Mission Sunday
>   15—Abraham Lincoln
>   22—The Meaning of Lent
> March   1—
>   8—
>   15—
>   etc.

The gaps were then closed in with topics which were felt to be of interest to the young people in question, such as "Boy and Girl Relations," "Choosing What to Read," "Our Denomination at Work in Many Lands."

4. Some societies *depend almost entirely on addresses by outside speakers.* This is in some respects an easy way to build programs, and it may provide a number of attractive and instructive evenings, but it leaves a good deal to be desired. The young people themselves are in grave danger of falling into "spectatoritis." They are entertained and enlightened from Sunday to Sunday, but they have all too little chance to do their own thinking and their own work,

and thus really to grow in Christian experience. The following are lifted out of such a program:

January	6—Address,	"Getting a New Start," by a seminary professor
	13—Address,	"God in Business," by a layman
	27—Address,	"God and Electricity," by a layman
February	3—Address,	"God and the Law," by a lawyer
	17—Address,	"Selecting a Mate," by the pastor
March	3—Address,	"God in Education," by a college professor

5. Some groups—one wishes their number were ten times greater—*develop their program on the basis of the several areas of the United Christian Youth Movement.* A quite natural procedure is to survey the various fields, begin with the one of greatest immediate interest, explore it in just the way that appeals most to the particular group in question, and then move on to another area. There is all the material a group could want for a year or two or three, and the guides contain innumerable suggestions for study, worship, and action.[4]

6. In a certain church it was decided that for a period of time its youth fellowship would *devote the first evening of each successive month to a chain of related programs, the second evening to another chain, and so on.* Thus the first Sundays of several months might be given to successive studies in the religions of the world; the second Sundays would take up the Bible from differing angles; the third Sunday would be "Current Events Night" with a consideration of the significance for Christian youth of recent happenings in the world; and the fourth Sunday would feature a musical program with the rendition of some fine instrumental music and the study and singing of a few of the

great hymns of the Church. Such a plan has the advantage of variety, but on the other hand it is rather discontinuous. It does not give a group a chance to take hold of a matter, and hang on until it has thought it through and acted it out.

7. In another church a brief series of meetings was used by the young people to *share with each other some personal Christian experiences*. What underlay this departure was the feeling that they had had an abundance of coldly rationalistic discussion, much talking about it and about, and now for a while something else was in order. The subjects for the four evenings of this experiment were:

> What Does Prayer Mean to Me?
> What Does Jesus Mean to Me?
> What Does Fellowship Mean to Me?
> What Does Winning Others Mean to Me?

They did not argue, for example, about what Jesus should mean to a young person; they gave personal testimony to what he did now mean and what he had meant to them. First of all, when they came together, there was a time of informal fellowship. Then followed a quiet service of worship throughout which their attention was riveted upon a reproduction of a painting of Christ. After this the way was opened for an unhurried "chipping-in" by this one and that one about what Jesus meant to him. A group would not want too many such sessions, but a few now and then might be a welcome change from mere hard thinking about the problems of life.

8. One young people's group set itself for as long as might be necessary to *develop a code for Christian living*. One by one the several areas in which a Christian is called upon to live out his faith were taken up, and these young people

tried to whittle out a series of statements which represented their best thought and their highest purpose. The eventual outcome was a highly compact two-page document, of which a brief sample is here given:

MY CHRISTIAN CODE

I. In my home now, I mean to—
1. Be a Christian healer of misunderstandings.
2. Have a spirit of helpfulness.
3. Develop a keener appreciation of parenthood.
4. Have a greater courtesy for and consideration of others

III. As a student, I shall—
1. Be co-operative with my instructors.
2. Endeavor to see their point of view.
3. Not let preconceived ideas influence me.
4. Be influenced by my instructors' quest for knowledge.
5. Refuse to cheat and do all in my power to cause the practice to cease.
6. Refuse to assist anyone during a test but do so afterwards.
7. Discourage fraternities and sororities and work toward a Christian fraternity.
8. Take my pastor into my confidence all through my student days.

9. A type of Sunday evening program which is both ambitious and churchly is the *Youth Church*. The congregation from which the following description comes has made a several-year trial of the Youth Church, and is well pleased with the results. An attractive bulletin describes the venture as follows:

The idea was conceived of providing an opportunity for the young people to come together and express their ideas concerning present-day problems and the application of Christianity to these problems. This has not only helped the young people to clarify their problems, but has enabled them to discover their relation to the church as well. At the same time, a closer understanding has been established between the older and the younger groups.

The official board of the church voted to suspend evening church services in order to make way for the Youth Church service, and to provide facilities for such an organization as well.

Each Sunday evening all groups assemble in Fellowship Hall for an opening devotional program forty-five minutes in length. There follow separate group meetings of forty-five minutes, the groups being divided as follows: junior—nine to eleven years of age; intermediates—twelve to fourteen years of age; senior—fifteen to seventeen years of age; young people—eighteen years and over. Adults are invited to the general assembly and to a class which meets at the same time as the group meetings. A social hour in Fellowship Hall for all groups follows the group meetings.

Candidates for membership in the Youth Church must take the following definite action: (1) Apply for membership to the official board of the Youth Church. The board meets the first Sunday of each month to receive members. (2) Accept and apply the Youth Church Covenant below [the covenant is then printed in full].

10. Closely akin to the foregoing in several important respects, but different in others, is the *University of Life*, which has been adopted in many churches and communities since its origin some seven years ago. This plan is featured by a long evening's session—two or three hours as a rule—and a balanced program. The four elements typically present are: a fellowship meal, a fellowship sing, worship, and simultaneous courses of study called "Interest Quests." The meal usually begins around half-past five o'clock, and is quite

inexpensive. The singing lasts perhaps twenty minutes, and closes with a hymn. The worship is conducted in the sanctuary itself, and is about thirty minutes in length—including a brief talk. The classes which follow run an hour in length, and a course requires six to ten of these hours. A variety of "Interest Quests" is offered, so as to appeal to all ages and groups of youth. Inasmuch as it is quite an undertaking to set up a "university" of such scope, the venture is often made jointly by several churches.

As to the results obtained, the University of Life is reported to have been successful in reclaiming young people who had lost touch with the Church, and also in reaching some who had never been in vital touch with the Church. By and large, it was found to be improving rather than detracting from the attendance of youth at the morning church service. By and large, it was improving church school attendance likewise, although it had the opposite effect in a minority of cases. The plan is copyrighted, but permission to use it can readily be secured from the Minnesota Council of Religious Education, St. Paul, Minnesota.[5]

This general type of Sunday evening program—long and balanced—by all appearances seems to be growing in favor throughout the country. Strange as it may seem, some young people may be remaining away from our Sunday evening meetings not because they are too long but because they are too short. They close at an awkward hour, and leave the young people "all dressed up and no place to go" for the remainder of the evening. It is for this reason that a longer program, if it has enough of variety in it, may meet with a hearty response in some cases.

11. An excellent way of developing a youth program—virtually unheard of fifty years ago, but widely used today—

is to *take hold of some interesting project and center all effort in it for a while.* This is the much discussed and much debated "project method," which after all is not so mysterious but a perfectly natural way for people to live and spend their time together. A group of youth simply get interested in some project or other—it may be the preparation of a drama, or the giving of friendly help to a group of migrant youth who drift into the community, or an investigation of how the second World War arose—throw themselves into this project, and along the way do whatever studying, or worshiping, or working with their hands seems necessary. That is about all there is to it. For example, the young people of one church undertook the novel experiment of presenting two plays on the same stage at the same time. The one represented one way of living; the other represented another; and the whole was entitled "Youth at the Crossroads." One hundred and fifty young people shared in this project from start to finish.[6] Now it is easy to conceive young people becoming enthusiastic over a venture of this sort, and it is easy to picture them—as they went along—doing some hard study, engaging in real worship, and performing much work with their hands. Their programs, therefore, for quite a number of weeks could center exclusively in this one project. Such an approach to program building requires ingenuity and hard work on the part of both young people and counselor, but it is worth it.

12. The freest possible way of shaping a program is to *cultivate a close fellowship in a youth group, and allow the program to grow from week to week as it will.* This may with some truth be called either the best way or the worst way—depending on circumstances. If there is an alert, resourceful advisor who is lightning-quick to seize upon leads

that arise and make the most of them, and if the young people are capable of disciplining their own life somewhat, it may be the best way. Otherwise, it is the worst way, for it is like the music that "goes 'round and 'round"—but comes out nowhere.

In the account which follows we see young people under wise guidance developing a group life which is natural, vigorous, and gets somewhere:

Starting with a gathering of an average of five young people each Sunday night in the parsonage, our Open House Fellowship has grown to a size that requires the use of the parish house. This fellowship was begun in a situation where there was no youth work outside of the church school department or class. The pastor quickly discovered that any attempt to introduce a formal type of youth work would sentence the effort to failure before it had a chance to begin. The only possibility seemed to be an informal setup in which fellowship would be the guiding principle for any activities sponsored by the group.

Since there is no evening worship service in the church proper, the young people arrive any time from 6:30 on, and leave any time they wish. A limit for leaving has been set by the group at 10:30 P.M. During this time the young people will play games, sing, play instruments, worship, read, do handicraft work, hike, discuss, etc. The main idea of the program is to take the young people with whatever interest they bring with them to the fellowship, and attempt to raise that interest to a religious level. Playing of games is encouraged not with the idea of winning, but to enjoy the fellowship of others. Reading done is of good literature placed there by the leaders. Music may begin in the secular but usually ends in the sacred vein. Discussions very often are the follow-up of a casual conversation of a small group of people.

This is guided and controlled by a simple organization. There are only temporary committees to do specific tasks, after the completion of which they are discharged with thanks. These specific tasks often serve as the basis for educating the group to be leaders.

There is only one place in the program where the entire fellowship is expected to co-operate as a group, and that is the service of worship. At all other times various activities may be going on simultaneously.

This list of an even dozen could easily be extended further, but there is no need of multiplying cases. If it does not cover everything that young people's societies and fellowships can do, it at least represents the chief program types and the chief approaches to program building.

METHODS OF WORK WITH YOUTH

WE HAVE THUS FAR in the consideration of our subject tried first of all to view sympathetically the young people who are our chief concern, and the circumstances of their life on the American scene. From this view we sought to derive some major objectives which we should like to achieve with them and for them—the "what" of youth work. From that we turned our attention to various questions of organization, and of proper provision for youth at the chief points in the Church's life—the church service, the church school, the youth society or fellowship. We are now ready to give our attention to the outstanding methods of work with youth. Methods are not cold abstractions, to be picked apart bit by bit as though they had nothing to do with living human beings. Instead they are the indispensable tools which we carry in our minds and in our hands and on our hearts as we approach Mary and John and their fellows to help them shape their lives after a worthy pattern. They are to us what saw and plane and hammer are to the carpenter. If we use these tools of our trade well, youth will be won and held to the Church and the Kingdom. If we use them poorly, youth will be lost to both Church and the Kingdom.

WORSHIP

We are thinking now not of youth's part in the corporate

worship of the congregation, but rather of their separate services of worship in church school and youth fellowship. At an earlier place the position was taken that these separate services of worship—especially those on Sunday morning—should be brief, so as not to detract from youth's attendance at the morning church service. Nothing that follows is to be taken as denying this position. Nevertheless, even though services be short, they need not be shoddy. Short or long, they deserve the best that we can give them.

Probably most of the questions which arise regarding the separate worship of youth can be gathered up under two main heads: first, planning for the worship experiences of youth over a period of time; and second, planning and carrying through an individual service. Let us look at these two in order.

First, then, *how shall we plan a year's program of worship with a youth group?* This very question implies that it is worth while trying to take a long view of youth's approaches Godward—and His approaches to them. Someone needs to see the worship experience of the year steadily, and see it whole—and plan for it. This "someone" may be the late summer retreat, of which we have previously spoken. There the first rough draft of the plans can be drawn. Later, in order to fill in the details, there may have to be a small committee, comprising the pianist perhaps and a very few other persons sensitive to beauty and trained in worship.

The plans thus drawn will ideally have a place for worship experiences of various sorts. The following types are rich with spiritual possibilities, and deserve to be represented:

1. A majority of conventional services of worship, relating very often to the study or project in which the group is engaged.

2. A limited number of special observances at Thanksgiving, Christmas, and the like—not entertainments but true worship.

3. A few joint services with other groups—a nearby youth fellowship, a group of another race, or merely other ages within the congregation.

4. One or more out-of-door services.

5. Several services employing symbolic rituals.

6. A service or so that is out of the ordinary, such as the Galilean service.

Some of these types are self-explanatory, but a further word may be in order concerning two or three of them. There is a crying need for joint worship with groups that are "different," alien, strangers, foreigners. At the great ecumenical conferences in Oxford, Edinburgh, Madras, and Amsterdam, where people of many faiths and tongues were assembled together, nothing so drew them into one fellowship in Christ as the experience of common worship. When they all stood in common need and adoration before the Father of all, then at last they knew themselves to be one. This same experience of unity in worship can be the happy possession of any youth group in any community—if they will but look ahead and make sure that it happens.

As to services out of doors in a beautiful natural setting, they afford youth a chance to approach the Creator through his handiwork, and they enable God to speak his own word to the souls of youth. Rural youth groups are particularly fortunate in this regard, and should make full use of their good fortune. Even city groups can have an Easter dawn service, and a summer vesper service or so. One youth fellowship from a small town held their worship one Sunday evening at a nearby-lake shore, the following week on a hilltop, and the third week from the highest mountain peak in the vicinity.

We have already indicated one use of symbolic rituals—namely, in connection with an annual service of installation of youth workers. But there are other occasions through the year when such rituals can make their lasting impression upon the senses and the emotions of youth. A running account of one youth group reveals four distinct times annually when the worship takes this form. The first is a communion service at the beginning of the fall term for youth alone, and adapted especially to them. The second is a "Hanging of the Greens" ceremony the second week before Christmas. With much merriment the young people decorate the room with greens, and then kneel before the open fireplace while Oxenham's "Sacrament of Fire" [1] is read and Christmas carols sung. The third is a candlelight service on the Sunday evening before Christmas. In a room lighted only by candles Van Dyke's "The Other Wise Man" is given by a talented reader year after year. The fourth is another communion service for youth, held quite appropriately on the first meeting night of each New Year.[2] As these services recur time after time, is it to be doubted that they grow in beauty and spiritual meaning for the young people who are privileged to be a part of them?

Mention has been made of the Galilean service as typifying "out of the ordinary" worship for youth. All such services run some risk of descending to the level of mere displays of talent and ingenuity, but they need not do so at all. They can be kept on the plane of true worship. There can, for example, be services centered in great art or great music which open a highway between man and God—as art and music have it in their power to do. To return to the Galilean service, it is nothing more nor less than a recounting in scripture, poem, and hymn of the earthly life of our Lord from its humble beginning to the glorious conclusion ascribed it by Christian faith. The worshipers can be invited in advance to let their minds dwell upon the majesty of this unfolding life, and its abiding meaning for present-day disciples. In the form here given—there are countless variants—all the necessary materials for the service are to be found in the Bible, *The Church School Hymnal for Youth* of the Westminster Press, *The New Hymnal for American Youth,* and Slack's anthology, *Christ in the Poetry of Today*.

A GALILEAN SERVICE

Silence
Instrumental Music: "Silent Night"
Scripture: Luke 2: 1-14—the birth of Jesus
Poem: "The Little Town"
Hymn: "Hail to the Brightness of Zion's Glad Morning"
Scripture: Luke 2: 40-52—the boy Jesus in the Temple
Solo: "Ye Fair Green Hills of Galilee"
Scripture: Matthew 3: 13-17—the baptism of Jesus
Hymn: "By Roads That Wound Uphill and Down"—a summary of our Lord's ministry
Scripture: Matthew 4: 18-22—Jesus calls his disciples
Hymn: "Jesus Calls Us"
Scripture: Matthew 5: 1-12—Jesus teaches on the mount
Solo: "O Son of Man, Our Hero Strong and Tender"
Poem: "There is a Green Hill Far Away"
Hymn: "Are Ye Able?"
Scripture: Luke 24: 1-8—the resurrection
Hymn of Triumph: "Jesus Christ Is Risen Today"
Poem: "The Poet"
Scripture: Philippians 2: 1-11—the challenge to us
Hymn: "Just as I Am, Thine Own to Be"
Instrumental Music: "O Jesus, I Have Promised"
Silence

We turn now to the second main question, *How shall we plan an individual service of worship with a youth group?* The adult adviser can of course do it all himself—perhaps better and more quickly than he could with a committee of young people. But he will miss a great joy if he does not often take youth into the service—both the preparation and the conduct of it. They are so quick to catch the essentials of true worship, so readily sensitized to what is beautiful and fitting, so eager to do their best, that it is a shame to rob them of their opportunity. The picture we have in mind, therefore, in what follows is an older counselor and perhaps three chosen young people putting their heads together to plan a youth service for a forthcoming session. The hour or so devoted to this may be broken down into a series of steps such as the following.

1. *Choose a theme.* A safe rule may perhaps be put in these words: Whatever will come to the minds of our group most naturally that morning—or evening—as the focal point of their communion with God, that should be the theme. It should not be picayunish; we have no business rushing into God's presence over trifles. It should not be artificial; we must come to him naturally, as children to a father. It should be something that he can legitimately be thought of as brooding over too, so that through it we may draw nigh to him. It may be the subject of our study or action at that time, or some high point in the church year, or a special day or season, or some community or world happening, or a deeply-lying need on the part of youth, or some aspect of the goodness and greatness of God himself.

2. *Select materials that fit the theme.* We have so much to draw from—hymns, prayers of many sorts, scripture read-

ings, poetry or meaningful prose, stories, pictures, instrumental music, the offering, calls to worship, responses to be said or sung. A few well-chosen source books of worship materials should be at hand to help at this stage of the work. If the young people are inexperienced, the adviser may list in advance a few prayers, and hymns, and especially scripture passages, from which their choice can be made. They will then not have to hunt aimlessly in books that are strange to them.

3. *Arrange these materials in proper sequence.* There is an order for worship of this sort which cannot safely be ignored. Young people are quick to grasp it, and to think in terms of it. Put quite simply, it runs as follows: (a) *The opening element or two should turn the thoughts of all Godward.* The first part of the service has no other necessary purpose but this. It may or may not be related to the theme that follows, but this one thing it must do. It may consist of a hymn such as "Spirit of God, Descend upon My Heart," or a scripture passage such as Psalm 100, or some other call to worship, or several of these. (b) *The second or third element announces unmistakably the theme of the service.* The worship leader does not make this announcement, but the service itself does. A well-chosen scripture reading, or a hymn, or a poem, or a story states so clearly that no one can mistake it what is the focal point of the worship of the hour. (c) *All that follows carries the worshipers from step to step in their thought and feeling about the theme.* This is the bulk of the service—perhaps two-thirds of it. The essential requirement is that it move naturally from stage to stage. For example, in a service of thanksgiving it is perfectly natural for the worshipers first to recognize God's goodness, then to express their thankfulness for his goodness, then to dedicate

themselves gratefully to his service. This order cannot easily be reversed. Hence, if the committee has found a poem which numbers God's mercies over one by one, and a prayer which offers our all in dedication to him, it is clear as can be in what order they should be arranged. (No mention is made here of the benediction or other appropriate ways of bringing the worship to a close. As a matter of fact, in many young people's sessions between the last-named material and the conclusion of the hour there intervenes a lesson or some other program, so that the worship proper actually ends as here indicated.) [3]

4. *Assign the several parts to those who will participate.* Some portions of the service will be more difficult than others—perhaps a poem of subtle meaning, or a scriptural passage with unfamiliar words and phrases. These can be given to the more capable members of the committee. The question here arises whether the leadership of worship should be divided among two or three persons, or retained in the hands of one. There are many who favor the latter alternative. On the other hand, if three young people know precisely what they are going to do, and sit close to the place where each in turn must stand, and perform their respective parts without announcement or any commotion whatsoever, the result can be entirely worshipful.

5. *Rehearse the parts as often as necessary.* Let each read over his part until all the hard words have been mastered, and the true meanings understood, and voice and manner perfected as much as possible. The adviser may sit near the rear of the room for this, in order to draw out clearness and distinctiveness of speech. Young people do not resent such discipline but rather welcome it, if the approach is transparently sincere.

In the foregoing outline there is one point that deserves a fuller treatment than it could receive within the outline itself. We have said simply, "Select materials that fit the theme," not specifying whether they are to be good, bad, or indifferent—so long as they fit the theme. But clearly a service of worship can rise no higher than the level of the materials that enter into its making. Hence a further word is needed concerning *worship materials*—both their *quality* and their *variety*.

As to their quality, we can never be too zealous in securing the strongest hymns, the most beautiful poetry, the most worthy prayers for the construction of our services. They cannot possibly be too fine, because we are offering them unto God himself. More than a hundred high school youth in summer camp were once asked to designate their favorite hymns. The five receiving the highest number of votes were:

"In the Garden"	12
"Follow the Gleam"	11
"The Old Rugged Cross"	9
"I Would Be True"	8
"Living for Jesus"	8

We do not wish to speak lightly for a moment of any hymn which has brought spiritual strength to any person; but two and perhaps three of these are what might be called hymns of sentiment; and, while the remaining two are fine and worthy hymns for youth, none of the five is drawn from the ancient musical treasury of the Christian Church. Why was this list as it was, and not different? Could it be that we are failing to "sell" some of our finest hymns, and prayers, and poetry to our youth?

As to the variety of such materials, the point to be made

is that there may be extremely valuable types of material beyond what we commonly employ—simply waiting to be used.   A hint of this appears clearly in the reactions of a number of church school pupils to a service which they had just experienced.   There were over six hundred of them between the ages of nine and twenty-three, and they had all participated in the same service—although in different places. The questions and answers which bear on our present point are as follows:

The people who planned this program arranged to have one idea running through all parts of it. (a) What do you think it was? (b) What makes you think so? Three highest answers to (b):

163—the story
58—the hymns
34—the prayer

Did you honestly think about God at any time during this service? If so, when? Three highest answers:

217—Yes, during the story
196—Yes, during the prayer
64—Yes, during the hymns

Would we have thought that the proper kind of story had such a potential value in worship?   How often have we made use of stories for worship purposes?   And so there may be lying just out of our present reach other types of worship materials which have been too long unused.   The field of visual aids is opening up rapidly; and there are drama, and symbolism, and ritualistic responses, and new uses of silence. Valuable books of worship suggestions are coming from the press almost monthly.[4]   There is scarcely any limit to what we can do except that set by the amount of time we have to give.

DISCUSSION

We turn now to a comparatively new method, and one which has effected a radical change in church schools and societies wherever it has gone. (It was developed largely by Professor H. S. Elliott, and any treatment of it cannot avoid drawing upon his pioneer thought at many points.) It now rests in our hands as a new and valuable tool, for whose help in our work with youth we may indeed be grateful. Let us approach it by endeavoring to deal with the chief questions which a youth worker might ask concerning it.

Under what circumstances is the discussion method usable? This would seem to be the first question to ask, for the reason that many of the failures with the discussion method have occurred while it was being attempted under the wrong circumstances. It is not a foolproof method, any more than any other. There are some things it will not do, and there are some conditions under which it will not work.

To begin with, then, *the discussion method is usable only for thinking through problems.* That is its rightful task. It is suited to that, as a saw is suited to cutting a board in two. Whenever the topic of a youth session can be cast in the form of a problem with a puzzling question mark at the end, then the discussion method may well be called upon. "What is the Christian stand in the present international crisis?" "How should boys and girls behave toward one another?" "Is gambling right or wrong?" All such questions it can deal with profitably and interestingly. It is not well adapted to teaching facts.

This line of thought suggests a brief detour into the subject of other teaching methods and their uses. It would be a mistake to assume that group discussion suddenly relegated all other methods to the scrap heap, like 1919 automobile models. They still hold an honorable place in teaching and learning—the individual report upon a topic of interest, the committee report, the study of printed materials, and the *lecture method*. As long as one person knows something which others do not know but want to know, we shall have need of the talk, the address, the lecture method. In general, this time-honored but much abused method may be said to have three principal uses. In the first place, it can convey facts and information. A person who knows the labor movement inside out, or a lifelong student of the book of Jeremiah, can lay the information he possesses before a group to their great good—provided they wish to know these particular facts. Second, it can report upon a significant experience. A judge who has served in a juvenile court for twenty years, or an observer at the League of Nations when the League was in flower, can "lecture" to good effect—provided his audience is interested in juvenile courts or the League of Nations. Third, it can present a significant point of view which the speaker himself holds with conviction. For example, a confirmed pacifist can make the case for nonviolence with great persuasiveness, or a convinced Christian can "proclaim the gospel" he professes with warmth and power. There are other uses of "lecturing," but these seem to be the chief ones.

Having completed the brief detour, we return now to the main road—namely, the circumstances under which discussion will work.

In the next place, *the discussion method is usable only when preceded by a talk, study, or experience—one or more of these three*.[5] When people meet to think together out loud—which is what discussion is—they must have something to think with. And where will they get this "stuff" for their thinking? Either some person must tell it to them, or they must look it up for themselves in books and journals and newspapers, or they must have come upon it in the course of their own experience. There do not seem to be any other ways.

Finally, *the discussion method is somewhat less usable with intermediates than with older youth.* The twelve- to four-teen-year-old will discuss, but not so long or so well as his older brother or sister. Stories, workbooks, and activities of various sorts must play a considerable part in the teaching of this age.

How does a person prepare to lead a discussion? This is the second question that is likely to perplex the worker with youth, and it is not an easy one. Next Sunday I am slated to lead a discussion on such and such a topic. What shall I do now as I sit in my home on Tuesday evening? If it were only a talk I could get ready for it—but a discussion! How can I know what is going to happen? What turn is it going to take? How can I prepare now to lead a discussion?

It is a bit puzzling the first time, and sometimes the hun-dredth time! For our example, let us suppose that the ques-tion to be discussed is, "How should a young person spend Sunday?" The adviser would be much easier in mind this Tuesday evening if he had sounded out the group briefly at their last meeting to discover the particular phases of this question which interested and perplexed them most. Lack-ing this, he is left to forecast as best he can the trend which the hour will take, and make his own plans accordingly. Conceivably, the sheet of paper before him in due time contains the following outline:

LEADER'S PREPARATION FOR A DISCUSSION ON
"HOW A YOUNG PERSON SHOULD SPEND SUNDAY"

1. Getting the chief problem into the open.

What are some of the things young people in our community do on Sunday? (This is an easy question, and will start the ball rolling.)

Expected answers: all the way from going to church to attending baseball games.

On which of these do people disagree chiefly?

Expected answers: dancing, all-day auto trips, and Sunday baseball—with this last striking fire most of all.

2. Getting proposals stated and weighed.

(In the matter of Sunday baseball the proposals state themselves—to patronize Sunday baseball, or not to patronize it. The important thing then, in this case, will be to get the proposals weighed.)

Why do some people object to Sunday baseball?

Expected answers: it interferes with church services, involves the handling of money, makes some men work seven days a week, violates the Fourth Commandment, etc.

Why do other people favor Sunday baseball?

Expected answers: Sunday is the only time some people can play or see games, baseball is wholesome outdoor recreation, doesn't conflict with church if confined to the afternoon, etc.

How did Jesus spend the Sabbath? Have someone read Mark 1: 21-35. (This will help them to weigh the matter more seriously than they have done.)

What ought Sunday contribute to our lives at any rate?

Expected answers: worship, religious instruction, rest, change, family fellowship, some time spent in nature, etc.

3. Getting a definite plan formulated.

In the light of the foregoing, shall we patronize Sunday baseball, or not? Are there any other things to do on Sunday which we have been neglecting? What ought to go into a Sunday program for Christian youth?

What can we plan in the immediate future as a group? As individuals?

This preparation—simple as it is—embodies the chief steps a prospective discussion leader must take. It will be noticed that the three headings contain three key words, each beginning with the same letter: problem, proposals, and plan. These are the three successive stages in all group thinking—problem, proposals, and plan. If a teacher or counselor will say them over and over to himself, fixing their meaning clearly, until they become second nature to him, he will have made a good start toward an understanding of the discussion process.

How does a person conduct a discussion? This is the third major question, which inevitably follows upon the other two. During the actual moments of the discussion what does one do? What is one supposed to do? What is the task of a discussion leader?

The sheaf of suggestions which follow are an attempt to give a compact answer to these queries:

THE TASK OF THE LEADER OF A DISCUSSION

1. To stimulate as many as possible to take part—
    a) The topic must be one of real concern to them, or must be made so.
    b) The atmosphere must be absolutely informal and natural.
    c) Especially at the start arrange it so that participation is easy—that is, ask easy questions and deal with phases of the subject that are "close home."
    d) Encourage those who have not participated. Recognize even trivial suggestions, coming from a person who has not hitherto taken part. Develop a "blind spot" for those who talk all the time.
    e) Help the group to set as one of its goals the mastery of the discussion method. Help them to see the difference between discussion and argument. Help them catch the

idea of short contributions, not long speeches—"kick the idea along." A few good-natured remarks about these matters are in order occasionally.

2. To keep the discussion "on the track"—

   a) Sometimes it is good to share with the group at the outset a tentative outline for their thinking—in terms of questions, not answers. "First we might take up this question, then this one," and so on. This serves as a road map, to give them some idea of where they are going.

   b) Use concrete cases wherever possible, rather than abstract problems. This helps to keep the discussion down to earth.

   c) Begin and end with action proposals, if possible. If the group has before it the necessity of actually doing something, it will be likely to stick to business.

   d) Sometimes a side issue *ought* to be followed up, instead of the original problem. It may mean more to the group. In such a case say, "Now, look here—we're off on this other question. Do we want to continue on it?"

3. To avoid heated arguments and emotional clashes—

   a) Much can be done by the leader's open-mindedness, even temper, and fairness to all concerned. Be particularly careful to give the views of an obstreperous minority a chance to get fairly stated. This takes the wind out of their sails, as it were.

   b) Begin with the less disputable phases of the question. Advance to the more disputable after a basis of mutual understanding and confidence has been laid.

   c) Think of the final solution in terms of an integration into which everybody's thinking has flowed rather than a victory of one solution over another—a "what" rather than a "which."

4. To keep the thought process moving along steadily and surely—

   a) Master the art of questioning. There are questions to

ferret out a problem; questions to get proposals stated, "what" questions; questions to get these proposals weighed, "why" questions; questions to discover plans of action, "how" questions.

b) Master the technique of the blackboard. Do not write everything down, but only key words and phrases. Use the same words given by the speaker. Do not comment every time.

c) Master the art of summarizing. Every now and then take inventory, especially when the discussion has lagged, or become cloudy. "It seems we are agreed on this and this, but the matters which still cause us trouble are this and this." Behold! a fresh start.

d) Master the art of recognizing whether the bar to further progress is a matter of available facts, or of judgment. If the former, get the facts. If the latter, think it through.

5. To get sufficient solid facts, biblical materials, etc., introduced—

a) For part of this the leader himself is responsible. He is two things: (1) a guide, a chairman; (2) an expert, a source of reliable information.

b) Pertinent materials should have been put in the hands of selected members or of the entire group beforehand. Collective ignorance does not equal knowledge.[6]

In the final analysis, the leadership of discussion must come to a person in the same manner as playing the pipe organ—namely, by hard study and long practice. The first venture or so may be utterly discouraging. But little by little the "feel" of it grows upon the youth worker, his confidence in himself and in the method grows apace, and at last he is in full possession of a new and useful tool for advancing the spiritual stature of youth.

RECREATION

When the young people in the Maryland study were requested to give the ways in which they spent most of their leisure time, a prominent place in the answers was taken by pure, unadulterated loafing. It stood fourth from the top of the list for the boys, and sixth for girls.[7] When these same young people were asked whether they felt their home communities offered sufficient recreational opportunities, about 70 per cent said "No" as against only 20 per cent who replied with a clear "Yes." [8] These two bits of statistics present the case for planned, wholesome recreation better than pages of abstract argument.

There is some comfort in the thought that this heavy responsibility does not rest upon the Church alone, but is shared by many community agencies. Certainly the Church should take into account what is being done by the public school, Y.M.C.A., Y.W.C.A., and the like, and avoid duplicating them or running competition with them. But in many communities there is a crying need for everything the churches can do in this regard. And in any case—no matter how extensive the programs of other agencies are—we shall want *some* of youth's good times to be spent under church auspices. It will not do to let them think that we are blithely unconcerned about that which concerns them so deeply. This would be the poorest way imaginable to win their affection and loyalty.

The Church's program of recreation for youth, then, deserves to be planned with as much care as its programs of worship and study. It may be a "minor," while these others are "majors," but it still merits careful planning. Perhaps the retreat—upon which we have staked our hopes in other connections—will attempt this task, taking into consideration what is being done by other agencies, what the young people truly need and enjoy, and what facilities are available. The plans will of course differ widely from church to church, but in general *a well-rounded church program of recreation for a year* will contain some or all of the types listed below. (It is encouraging to note how many of these require no elaborate equipment. The games and activities of the gymnasium can of course be added for those so fortunate as to possess one. But none of the following items requires costly building and equipment. A church basement, a small anteroom, a church lawn, a near-by field, a deserted barn, the homes of the members, and the general resources of the community—all of these can be pressed into service.)

1. *Indoor parties.* The "sociable" has long been a mainstay of the recreational program, and young people still enjoy it—provided it is interesting, novel, and so well planned that there are no awkward gaps or delays. Literally hundreds of party programs are in print on themes that fit every season of the year, and the possibilities are not yet exhausted. An experienced recreational leader with youth has designed a party program which—with some modifications—is briefly outlined here to exemplify the principles that underlie a good party program.

A JANUARY SOCIAL

(Among other things, January stands for the making of resolutions. Why not have, therefore, "A New Year's Resolution Party?")
1. Resolved to travel more widely: the familiar game "Going to Jerusalem."
2. Resolved to make more friends: "Come with me."
   Circle formation, facing toward center. Leader walks around circle on inside, takes any player by the hand, and

says, "Come with me." Immediately the new person joins the leader, but also reaches for another player, saying, "Come with me." Continue until about ten players are in the procession. Then leader drops a bunch of keys or blows a whistle and all try to get back to circle, the last one being "it" for the next time. Play six or seven rounds.

3. Resolved to know more famous people: "Who am I?"

Pin slips of famous persons, dead or living, on the backs of players, and have each guess the name on his back by listening to the other players talk to him as if he were that person.

4. Resolved to be a better speller: "Spelling bee."

Raise right hand for A; left hand for E; point to eye for I; point to open mouth for O; point to others for U.

5. Resolved to get more exercise: Grand march.

6. Resolved to pass all examinations:

You pass according to what you wear. Leader names something he is to wear at examination. Next the player on leader's right names an object of dress, and so on. If a player names an object worn by the person on his right, the leader states that he will pass. Keep going around the circle until almost all have caught on.

7. Resolved to eat lightly: Refreshments—not too light.

8. Resolved to do more singing: Group sing, tapering off to Negro spirituals and a religious closing.

Looking over this program point by point, one can find hidden within it the basic principles on which all good party planning rests.[9] One will notice, for instance, that the first game is easy, thus inviting all present to take part heartily. One will see also that there is alternation of active and quiet games—not too many of either kind in a continuous stretch— and a good deal of variety throughout the program. Further, one will notice that something is planned for the period after the refreshments. The evening is not allowed to peter out ignominiously in a shuffle of chairs, paper plates, and dirty napkins. Finally, since this program is planned for church groups, it closes on the religious note. Such a closing need not strike anyone in attendance as strange if the transition from general hilarity to a quieter mood is skillfully done. There is no better way of making this transition than through singing.

2. *Outdoor good times.* Little need be said about this form of recreation, except that it can be recommended to city youth because they do not live much in the open, and to country youth because they do live in the open. For the former it is a welcome and healthful change. For the latter it is merely taking advantage of opportunities close at hand. The possibilities are almost unlimited—hikes of many kinds, mountain climbing, athletic games, field meets, water sports, sledding parties, hayrides, outdoor meals, periods of camping, and so on. Every year's program of recreation should include a fair sprinkling of these. Unlike some other types of good times, they are as attractive to intermediates as to older young people.

3 *Hobby groups.* These represent one of the most promising leisure-time activities for our day. If there is any one of these six that needs to be stressed, this is the one. For hobbies demand little equipment as a rule; they are suited to small groups and even to lone individuals; they fill in constructively hours that might be wasted or worse; they are equally well suited to the junior high school and the college age; and—most important of all—they can be carried on into adulthood and even old age. These are some of the reasons why church youth groups do well to think more and more about "the care and feeding of hobbyhorses," as a booklet title expresses it.

One good way of stirring up interest in hobbies is to have

a "Hobby Show," at which young people—and others—are asked to display their favorite collections, skills, and interests.   One such show brought together such a fascinating array as the following: quilts, hooked rugs, crocheted pieces, cream pitchers in the shape of a cow (all of them blue), Indian relics, photography, an art scrapbook, minerals, old books, animals carved from soap, dolls representing strange types of people in our own country and other lands, and antiques.[10]   This is enough to make a person's mouth water. The evening began with the showing of a three-reel film, "We Are All Artists," and it doubtless closed with the making of numerous resolutions to take up this or that hobby.

4. *Liquorless dances, refreshment stands, and night clubs.* This new development owes its rise to the turn of events since prohibition was repealed.   Young people—church youth included—have gravitated toward cocktail bars, commercialized dance halls, and unsavory night clubs in such numbers that something had to be done.   The most logical thing to do was to give these places a run for their money by setting up counterattractions, completely dry and decent yet interesting.   The result has been almost a movement, spontaneously arising in different localities, which constitutes a fine tribute to both the devotion and the ingenuity of youth workers. The names of these ventures are intriguing; "Bar None," "Milk Shake Night Club," and "Dry Dock" are among the best.   They are sponsored by student groups, by churches, by the social agencies of a community working co-operatively, and by individuals who see a chance to turn an honest penny and do good at the same time.   They proceed on the sound assumption that it is scarcely enough to berate young people for attending places of low standards; they must be given something better.   Not all church groups of youth can or

should undertake ventures of this sort, but some will doubt-less feel impelled to do so.

This brings us to the edge of a question that is never far from the surface when church-centered recreation for youth is being discussed—the question of dancing, card playing, and the like under church auspices. In some churches today this issue is a frequent source of tension between the two genera-tions. About all that can be said is that each age should make an honest effort to see how the matter looks to the other. If the young people can fully appreciate how their parents were reared, and how it would hurt them to see the an-nouncement of a dance sponsored by a church group, they may decide that the hurt to their parents outweighs the en-joyment they would get from the dance—and drop the matter. Furthermore, they may agree that they have many other opportunities to dance and play cards, and their church socials can broaden their repertoire, so to speak, and teach them not to be dependent on one or two activities alone for a good time. On the other hand, if the adults see how large a part cards and dancing play in the social life of present-day youth, and how much these activities mean to them, and the kind of place they will frequent if the church does not broaden its policy, they may decide to swallow hard, take a deep breath, and make the plunge for the sake of their young people.

5. *Hearty participation in the celebration of community festivals.* This may not seem at first to belong under the head of a church program of recreation, but there is real en-joyment and fellowship in a Fourth of July picnic or a Colum-bus Day pageant. We must not think of recreation too nar-rowly. During the Middle Ages the great festival days were the high points in the community's life year after year, the

chief times when the life of the community overflowed its usual bounds and obliterated the cruel landmarks of poverty, labor, sickness, and death.   In our modern world likewise these community festivals may be high points of the year, in which church youth groups can have a part along with many others.   The production of a great Thanksgiving pageant with its script writing, rehearsals, scenery making, advertising, and final presentation can provide the finest sort of "recreation" for many individuals and groups.

Best of all, this type of recreation is open to small churches as well as large, country churches as well as urban, churches without equipment as well as those fully equipped.   Some years ago several rural communities in a midwestern state prepared an all-year recreational program which received considerable publicity.[11]   When this program is analyzed, it is found to consist largely of the very sort of thing best suited to communities lacking extensive equipment—namely, hobby or interest groups of many sorts, and an amazing number of special celebrations.   There are about twenty of these latter, including Halloween, Armistice Day, Thanksgiving, Christmas, New Year, Washington's Birthday, St. Patrick's Day, Easter, May Day, and a community fair.

6. *A few joint fellowship activities with "different" groups.* There are the same good reasons for playing with those who are different from us as there are for worshiping with them. A year's program of recreation for any youth group, therefore, is incomplete if it never reaches out beyond the group itself. It should on at least a few occasions widen the fellowship to include others in the congregation, or the young people of a near-by church, or a youth group of some other nationality or race, or a number of underprivileged children.   A certain college fraternity has for years held a Christmas party for

neighborhood children whose Christmas joys might otherwise be very meager. This is "recreation" for the children
and for the students, but recreation which has taken on a new
dimension. Such "fourth dimension" recreation is entitled
to a secure place in the planning of all church youth.

As just intimated, activities of this sort shade over almost
imperceptibly into service to others. They are held not only
with others, but for others. We are led, therefore, quite naturally into the next method which we wish to consider.

SOCIAL ACTION

The place of social action in a Christian youth program
should require no defense. It is called for by the dire needs
of the world around us, wherein people without number are
starving, suffering, hating, fearing, and dying. But it is called
for just as urgently by the needs of church young people
themselves. They need social action for the sake of their own
souls. Without it they can never know the height and the
breadth and the length and the depth of the Christian life;
their Christian experience is a sadly mutilated thing, like
an otherwise beautiful tree with the top third hacked out.
Likewise, without social action the life of a youth fellowship
is mutilated and sadly incomplete. Perhaps this is the trouble with some of our youth groups; this may be why they
are so lifeless, uninspired, and uninspiring—they rarely get
around to actual costly Christian living in a real world. It
might be that some of our half-dying youth organizations
would get a new spark of vitality and even increase their attendance if they let themselves give as much attention to social action as to worship, study, and recreation.

Despite the supreme importance of proper social action,
most of us engaged in youth work would probably confess

that this is the very point about which we know the least and at which we have done the least. Social action deserves to be planned for and carried out in the year's program with exactly the same thoroughness as worship, study, and recrea· tion; but have we done so? If the answer to this question is what it seems to be, here is the point at which we need to concentrate much of our devotion this year and the next. Let us approach the matter by endeavoring to ask and partially answer a few of the questions that arise immediately.

First of all, *what can a youth group actually do?* By way of answer, it may be helpful to bring together in one place the various kinds of action which are open to us. Different classifications can be given, and have been given. The following, if not complete, may at least be suggestive—some could be performed by intermediates; others only by older youth:

1. Acts of service to our own home church:
   Ushering.
   Helping to print the church bulletin.
   Distributing church bulletins or letters.
   Contributing systematically to the church's support.
   Making specific contributions for definite needs or equipment.
   Seeking to win other youth to full church membership (evangelism).
   Assuming a clear-cut responsibility in any project which the church undertakes, from soliciting funds to cleaning out vice spots.
2. Acts of service to needy individuals:
   Financial relief to underprivileged families.
   Food and clothing to underprivileged families.
   Friendly services to the helpless—cutting wood, sewing, caring for the children of employed mothers, etc.

Companionship to the lonely—Christmas caroling to shut-ins, open house to migrant youth, simple friendly visits.

Vocational counseling and assistance to the unemployed.

Recreational first aid to the unoccupied.

3. Active support of our own denomination:

Faithful, generous contributions to the denomination's budget.

Specific gifts and services—to orphanages, hospitals, educational institutions, student foundations, mission stations.

4. Active support of worthy agencies and movements—both money and time:

The Red Cross.

Local social service organizations.

Law and order societies.

Fellowship of Reconciliation, and other peace groups.

Temperance societies.

The co-operative movement.

The organized labor movement.

5. Firsthand investigation of actual conditions:

Housing.

Recreational facilities.

Health.

Unemployment.

Migrants.

Working conditions—hours, wages, tenure, safety precautions, etc.

Delinquency and crime.

Discrimination against Negroes, Jews, "foreigners."

Relief—governmental and private.

6. Ventures in fellowship and understanding:

Intervisitations and joint projects with Roman Catholics, Jews, Negroes, other nationalities, the other side of the tracks.

7. Actually tackling conditions that injure human beings:

Starting a co-operative or credit union.

Building a swimming pool or community center.

Getting out the vote against Sunday movies.

Campaigning against obscene literature.

Patronizing restaurants that do not sell liquor.

Circulating reliable movie estimates for the guidance of movie-goers.

Giving wide publicity to housing conditions, for example.

Starting self-help employment projects for the unemployed.

Touring the country as a "Peace Caravan."

The only purpose that an outline such as this can serve is to suggest in what directions to look for things to do. A retreat or a planning group of any kind might survey all the possibilities herein contained as it lays out the program for the coming year. In order further to "prime the pump" with ideas of what can be done, we list here a few books and pamphlets which contain stirring accounts of action projects actually carried through, as well as detailed proposals for others.

F. W. Herriott, *Christian Youth in Action* (The Friendship Press, 1935) —accounts of what has been done; suggestive and stimulating.

P. R. Hanna, *Youth Serves the Community* (D. Appleton-Century Company, 1936) —the same, coming from the public school field.

E. L. Shaver, *Church School Projects* (The University of Chicago Press, 1924) —the same, not all of them projects of social action.

W. N. Hutchins, *Graded Social Service for the Sunday School* (The University of Chicago Press, 1913) —the programs of a number of church schools described.

The several pamphlets developed by the United Christian Youth Movement (The International Council of Religious Education) —these embody suggestions not merely for study and worship but also for action.

Materials such as these not only provide ideas, but set a

sensitive reader on fire. A few of them would make a good investment for any youth group.

A second question arises at once—namely, *How relate such action to the other parts of the program?* In common practice the ventures in service and social rebuilding of youth groups have often borne no particular relation to their study and worship. Such unrelated activities may do much good, and they are not to be despised for one moment. Ideally, however, we should like to see study, worship, social action—and perhaps even recreation sometimes—all bound up into one bundle. The study might lead to action (for example, a study of missions) ; or the action might lead to study (for example, the starting of a co-operative) ; or worship might lead to action (for example, a deeply moving Armistice Day service). The curricular materials now being prepared for youth work often provide for just such a concentration of the entire program upon one theme. Many present-day quarterlies do so, and the pamphlets of the United Christian Youth Movement program are really study-worship-action pamphlets because they often contain suggestions side by side for all three.

A third and very difficult question is: *How does one plan and carry through a project of social action?* There are steps in a worship service, and in group discussion, and in a party; are there steps and stages likewise in planning and carrying out some piece of social action?

In a certain sense no such steps can be found in this case, because each activity is so different from all others. But in another sense, there is a general pattern which the youth worker can bear in mind as he approaches such a project. In order to illustrate them, let us take a very simple example. Let us imagine a high school group planning some help to a needy family at Christmastime. As the teacher looks ahead to this friendly venture, and as he carries it through with his class, he may keep such questions as the following in mind:

1. How shall I get this activity started? Ideally the initial suggestion would come from the class itself, but suppose it doesn't; then what?

   Perhaps our course of study can be made to suggest it.

   Perhaps our worship can be made to suggest and inspire it.

   The method of "exposure" may be best:

      The reading of some cases from Calkins, *Some Folks Won't Work.*

      A visit and talk by a social worker.

      Best of all, a visit on our part to certain streets or roads.

2. What organization will be needed to carry it through?

   Merely several informal committees:

      One to make a visit—if all of us cannot go.

      One to do the necessary purchasing.

      Etc.

3. What action possibilities does it contain?

   The visit, or visits.

   Doing chores at home to raise money for the purchases.

   Possibly a class money-raising project.

   Making our own toys for the children and gifts for the parents.

   Getting and trimming a Christmas tree for the family.

   Interviewing a social worker to discover how widespread such need is.

   Shopping in grocery stores, clothing stores, and the like.

4. What study possibilities does it contain?

   Why are there rich and poor people?

   What does poverty do to people?

   What measures is our community taking to relieve poverty?

   How should a Christian use his money—at Christmas and other times?

Biblical passages bearing upon stewardship, social justice, etc.

The lives of people like Jane Addams who devoted themselves to those in need.

5. What worship possibilities does it contain?

A service of gratitude to God for his good gifts.

A service of remembrance of those in need.

A service celebrating Jesus' ministry of helpfulness.

A service dedicating what we have and what we are to Christian service.

6. What Biblical passages would be appropriate to this activity?

Jesus' parables concerning money and its use.

Jesus' teaching concerning the infinite worth of a human being.

The book of Amos on social justice.

The book of James on wealth and poverty.

7. At what points must I watch it to insure the finest outcomes?

They should finish whatever they start.

Their attention should be centered all the while on the people with whom they are sharing Christmas joy; not on their own righteousness in doing this.

They should give help wisely; not merely sentimentally.

They should see this activity not as an isolated event, but as an integral part of the coming of the Kingdom.

These seven questions apply equally well to helping a needy family, starting a co-operative, or giving support to missions. In no case will all of the possibilities envisioned be realized, but the proportion will be larger if they are seen clearly ahead of time.

The three problems thus far dealt with are probably the major ones to arise in the mind of a youth worker concerning social action. However, there are a couple of auxiliary questions which demand attention also.

How shall we handle the finances of our youth group?

Money is time and effort and energy boiled down into little pieces of metal or paper. Wherever our money goes, we go; whatever it does, we do. Therefore, the generous giving and wise spending of money is a true part of a program of social action.

Perhaps the first rule for a youth group in this regard is that it should have a conscientiously thought out budget. One fellowship reports simply that "the annual budget is around $400, exclusive of the weekly publication which is financed by the church school. This is expended in a varied program of activities. Close to $100 is sent each year to the missions program of our church. Another $60 is used in local social service work. Young folks are assisted financially to attend the summer institutes of our denomination."

Further, a part of the giving—it seems—should be for highly specific objects. This means the purchase of a piece of chancel furniture, in addition to assisting faithfully with the budget of the local church; a part of the salary of some missionary who has gone out from the home community, in addition to contributing to missions; help to a family whose names and faces and sorrows and joys are known to the group, in addition to supporting the Community Chest drive. Not all giving should be of this sort, but some of it should be. Both general and specific giving are needed.

How shall we handle missions in our youth group? It goes without saying that church youth groups should devote hard study to missions—the dramatic history of this enterprise from the early apostles to the heroic saga of Chinese missionaries today, the particular program of a given denomination, the reasons for missions in our day and the types of missionary effort most sorely needed. Beyond this there should be many firsthand contacts with the field through pictures, letters, and visits of missionaries. And beyond this—and here we come to true social action—there is needed actual participation in this great cause through sacrificial, specific giving. This word "specific" meets us once again, and rightly so; for it holds the clue to making missions come alive for our young people. If they can "stake a claim" for five dollars or a hundred dollars in the evangelistic journeys of some man whom they know intimately, or in a hospital the pictures of which cover their own bulletin board, or in a scholarship for some young national who has visited their own fellowship, they may begin to catch something of the strange passion which has sent men and women to the uttermost parts of the earth. Alongside of this "claim-staking," some of their money can flow into the regular denominational missionary channels to identify them with the whole enterprise—but not all of it.

DRAMA

The four methods which we have thus far discussed are undoubtedly the "big four" of young people's work in the church. However, there remains yet another which is important enough to deserve separate treatment. As a matter of fact, it is an invaluable aid in each of these four major methods. Drama can be used with telling effect in worship. There are altar and chancel plays especially designed for such use. It can be utilized also as an adjunct of study and discussion. Such a book as *Looking at Life Through Drama*[12] employs dramas to open wide several of the most troublesome issues confronting youth today. It is equally useful for purposes of recreation, as many a church knows from happy experience. And it can even be turned to the purposes of social action. What better way is there for a youth group to strike a blow against war than through the production of a good peace play?

It is both encouraging and challenging to survey the true story of the results achieved in one small church by a year's earnest dramatic effort. If this account whets the interest of some youth group who have thus far made little use of drama, and impels them to read new books and launch new ventures, it will have served its purpose.

While it is practically impossible in a small congregation with a limited number of young people to achieve all that drama advocates declare, here in our church through scattered efforts we have been enjoying a few of the benefits. Looking back at our humble attempts of one year, we see the following results.

1. *A definite drama consciousness.* Most of us live far away from the centers of the legitimate theater, and thus part of our general educational development is neglected. This first, therefore, I consider a valid and valuable acquisition for both our actors and the audience.

2. *Progress in speaking ability.* It is a pleasure now to see some of our young people leading a worship service, standing before people with ease and assurance, and holding the attention of the congregation. Through drama they've learned to speak clearly, enunciate properly, pronounce correctly, and appreciate the beauty of the English language.

3. *Increase in the powers of observation and of sympathy for others.* To portray their various roles, the young people have been challenged to observe human nature, to note how men and women act and react in daily life, to see people as human beings and not as social security numbers. At the same time, through a study of the play characters, they have developed a sympathy and understanding for other people. Having to place themselves in others' shoes, to see through others' eyes, and to think others' thoughts has been a healthy and rewarding exercise.

4. *Material contributions to the congregation's life.* Because of financially successful productions the drama group has given

to the congregation: substantial contributions toward debt reduction; a complete set of glass partitions separating their department from others in our social room; beautiful shrubbery for the front of the church building; drama books to the church school library; their dramatic talent in congregation-wide programs at Christmas, Children's Day, and other similar occasions, as well as for our social and money-raising activities.

5. *In short* . . . . I'm glad we've had dramatic activities in our little congregation. I am convinced that they have added immeasurably to our common happiness, and have contributed to a unity of spirit and endeavor and hope.

One of the reasons why more youth groups do not make consistent use of the dramatic method is the lack of equipment. It is worth while, therefore, to point out that there is scarcely any church which need be held back from presenting plays on this score. There may, for example, be no stage. But if there is as much as a single church school room in addition to the church sanctuary, the platform there can be enlarged into a permanent stage. And, if the worst comes to the worst, a knock-down platform can be constructed and used as needed. Other items of equipment can be improvised in an amazing manner. For instance, one manual [13] describes how drapes of an inexpensive sort can be made to serve as backdrops, how portable footlights can be rigged up on two boards placed at right angles lengthwise, how a rheostat can be devised from a bucketful of salt water, how a passable oriental lamp can be shaped from a potato, and how the howling of wind and the flash of lightning can be simulated from materials to be found in any garage. Nor does such homemade equipment necessarily spell shoddy plays. It need not do so, and it must not do so. There is nothing worse than a bad play, and the record of church groups in this regard is none too good. Our church plays should be highly finished products—whether our equipment be improvised or the last expensive word.

By and large there are two chief requisites for a good dramatic production, and only two. The first of these is *a good play*. If the play itself is poorly constructed, no amount of equipment or rehearsals can remedy this defect. There are many excellent sources of materials, from which catalogues and annotated lists can be secured on request.[14] Beginning with the September, 1936, issue the *International Journal of Religious Education* under the heading "A Dramatic Calendar for Churches" published lists of dramas suitable to the several months, compiled by H. A. Ehrensperger. The question inevitably arises, Shall a royalty or a nonroyalty play be chosen? There are, of course, admirable nonroyalty plays, but the widespread tendency to shy away from royalty plays has been on the whole a great misfortune. Five or ten dollars spent on a royalty may turn out to be the best sort of investment.

The second requisite for a good production is *a good director*. For this too there is no substitute. Consequently great care should be exercised in the selection of the person who is to guide the venture to the final presentation. Fortunately many public school systems contain at least one person who is qualified to assume this responsibility. Also an increasing number of young people are receiving valuable training in college dramatic groups, and are making their way back into communities both large and small.

These are the only two requisites that are truly essential. If they are cared for, the rest will not take care of itself, but can be taken care of by dint of ingenuity and hard work.

As to the actual technique of drama production—the casting of players, the rehearsals, and the like—that is a matter to be discussed at some length by those who are true dramatic specialists. Excellent manuals are available for those who desire them. The book already mentioned is one of the simplest and best. It treats the subject in a manner quite helpful to large and small churches alike.

In view of the many values inherent in the preparation and presentation of plays, a youth group may well plan to give a definite place to drama in each year's work—one or two or more first-class productions each year. In so doing, it will be benefiting its congregation and community; it will be benefiting its own members individually; and it will be benefiting itself. Sometimes a play affords just the rallying point a group needs to pull its membership together and give it a new lease on life. For this as for other purposes it is often true that "the play's the thing."

VIII

THE WORKER HIMSELF

WE HAVE SPOKEN of program and methods as though they were all-important and all-sufficient, but in the final analysis methods of work are secondary to the worker himself. It is the worker who must make the methods work. And it is the Christian faith and life of the worker which must finally quicken a like faith and life in the young people with whom he works. We dare never forget that Christianity began not with a program or a handful of methods, but with the Word becoming flesh and dwelling among men. This manner of beginning must in a sense be repeated afresh in each new generation. One life—in this case, that of the adult teacher or counselor—must catch up something of the boundless love and gracious purpose of God, and pass it on to other and younger lives. One of the chief reasons for using methods is that they give this a chance to happen. When all is said and done, all methods depend for their effectiveness upon the skill and the Christian integrity of the worker.

HIS PERSONAL QUALIFICATIONS

Who is the good worker with youth? What kind of person must he be? What qualities of mind and heart and hand should he possess in order to be a workman unashamed?

For an answer to these questions we can scarcely do better than to consult young people themselves for their ideas on the matter. Their judgment is not final, but it is final for them. The way they feel determines whether or not they will come and keep on coming. And often they have an uncanny ability to size up what a given worker truly is, and what any worker ought to be.

In a recent summer school the young people assembled there were asked to register their judgments in this regard on a questionnaire which was supplied them. Their answers deserve to be pondered carefully by all who aspire to work with youth. Inasmuch as there are significant differences between the age groups, the replies of the several ages are given separately. It is interesting to speculate how a group of intermediates might reply.

HOW YOUNG PEOPLE FEEL TOWARD ADULTS WHO WORK WITH THEM

1. From among all the adults who have worked with you since you were twelve years of age in the church or any other religious organization—church school teachers, ministers, society counselors, club leaders, etc.—select the one or two who have meant most to you and helped you most in your religious development. What was it about this person (or persons) that made him such a good worker with youth? *In the following list check the three items (no more and no less) which best give the answer to this question:*

	15-17	18-23	Over 23	Total
Sense of humor	17	9	8	34
Splendid Christian character	24	23	11	58
Thorough knowledge of the Bible	1	2	3	6
Likable personality	20	12	6	38
Sincere devotion to the Church	9	4	5	18
Deeply religious spirit	2	4	1	7
Alibity to understand and get along with young people	30	29	4	63
Fine skill in teaching or leading a group	14	15	1	30

Strong body, well-trained in athletics.	6	0	0	6
Interest in the things young people are interested in	30	14	4	48
Good education	5	1	4	10
Capacity for friendship with individuals	12	7	4	23

2. In your estimation where do adult workers with young people fall down chiefly? *In the following list check the three items (no more and no less) which best give the answer to this question:*

	15-17	18-23	Over 23	Total
Too old to get along well with young people	19	5	1	25
Don't know enough about the things they try to teach us	14	11	11	36
Don't practice what they preach	11	13	4	28
Too young to command our respect ..	2	1	0	3
Boss us too much	16	14	6	36
Aren't really and truly interested in religion	5	3	2	10
Don't put enough time on preparation	14	12	8	34
Don't genuinely like young people ...	7	8	4	19
Don't attend regularly	7	2	4	13
Opposed to our having good times...	11	7	1	19
Too quick to criticize us	29	27	6	62
Old-fashioned in their points of view.	29	17	4	50

Here we see ourselves as young people see us. The quality in us which they value above all others is "an ability to understand and get along with young people." And the point at which we fail chiefly in their eyes is our readiness to criticize them. Apparently they do not care a great deal how old we are—the high school youth are considerably more sensitive on this point than the others—but they care immensely how old-fashioned we are. They value highly "a splendid Christian character" on our part, but are not particularly concerned about our athletic ability or the number of degrees we hold from institutions of learning. They would like us to be interested in the things which interest them, to be friendly to them, to have a sense of humor, and to refrain from bossing them. Bossing they cannot stand. In addition to all this, they would like us to be likable, and to know something about the things we try to teach them.

This is not an unreasonable set of demands—not at all! It is no more than they have a right to expect of us, and we should expect no less of ourselves.

His Dealings with a Group

Normally an adult worker must deal with a group of young people, and a group is a living, breathing thing. Each group has a personality of its own. Whatever its nature, the adult worker must deal with it. He must take it as it is, and help it to become the best it can be. Every September, it may be, he faces this problem afresh. He wants to develop a group morale, an *esprit de corps*. He wants a strong group, a happy group, an active group. He wants the members to enjoy being together, and doing things together. He wants a group life out of which a vigorous program will keep emerging constantly, like a fountain rising constantly from its source. How can he accomplish these ends? Among all the things that he can do, what will best promote a group consciousness of this sort?

There is, of course, no one answer to this question. Hearty recreational programs, especially around the opening of each new year of work, will help to bind a group together. But the young people who are bound together only by good times are not bound very tightly.   Another strategy for getting a strong group spirit under way is to discover a few key young people, and make them the rallying center for the group's life.   One experienced youth worker prefers this method to the more conventional way of holding a stirring rally to give the group an initial push.[1]   This is doubtless an excellent way of beginning, but then what?   How shall the group morale be kept high month after month?

The deepest secret of a strong and happy group seems to be contained in one word, *democracy*.   The worker who is willing to be democratic in all his dealings with his group, to respect each member of it as he himself desires to be respected, to encourage each boy and girl to play as large a part as age and ability will allow, to help and advise and counsel but never to dictate—such a worker will find a wholesome group personality developing before his eyes.   Let us see whether this is so, and how it is so.

Democracy allows each member of the group to have a real part in its life.   No one is left out.   No one is squelched.   Each young person is permitted to have his say and do his part.   Thus he becomes interested in the group.   He comes to have a stake in it.   It is his own.   He has put something of himself into it.   He is a part of it, and it is a part of him.   In this way democracy makes for a fine group life.

Democracy permits each member of the group to become truly acquainted with the others.   Theoretically twenty young people could meet in the same room every Sunday evening for five years hand running under an autocratic regime, and never get to know one another.   There they would sit night after night, each one locked up securely in his own shell.   No true opinions would be expressed, no personalities released from the shell.   How could they come to know one another under such conditions? But under democracy personalities come out of their shells—to know and be known. Ties of mutual understanding are woven around and among a number of personalities, until they are finally one group. In this way democracy makes for a fine group life.

Democracy dodges many of the resentments that autocracy piles up among members of a group. It is easy to believe that under a strong, autocratic hand people are prone to become resentful and tense, and to "take it out" on one another. Human nature being what it is, that is about what one might expect to happen. We now have some striking confirmation that it does actually happen. A number of boys' clubs were put at one time under autocratic control, and at another under democratic control. Under the former the boys during a given period "took it out" on one another in 185 acts of enmity, unkindness, criticism, and the like; under the latter there were only five such acts.[2] In the former instance they could have no true group life, because resentments tear a group to pieces as effectively as a demolition bomb. In the latter instance there could be a happy sense of togetherness. In this way democracy makes for a fine group life.

Democracy alone keeps a vigorous program emerging out of the life of a group. An attractive program can be imposed upon a group under autocracy, or provided for them, but it cannot spring up out of the group's life itself. Only democracy will permit that—the personality of the group expressing itself, as it were. In order to have that happen, there must be cabinet and committee meetings at which the adult counselor assists but does not preside. There must be discussions which he enriches but does not dominate. He is a coach on the side lines, an unfailing source of ideas and suggestions, an eagle-eyed discerner of false leads, a patient guide in the process of weeding out the false from the true; but he is not a dictator, nor an autocrat, nor even a leader. He is the servant—not the slave—of his group. He does the things they can't do; he suggests the plans they can't visualize; he sees the difficulties they can't see without his aid; he lends them of his own supply of persistence and faith when they are ready to quit. But he makes no more decisions than are necessary, says no more than necessary, does no more than necessary, and his greatest joy is to watch them becoming more and more able to get along without him. Under such a regime a vigorous program will be free to well up out of the group itself, and in this way democracy makes for a fine group life.

His Dealings with Individuals

In the final reckoning the concern of an adult worker with youth is centered in individuals one by one. It is for their sakes that the group and its program exists; it is for their sakes that he plans and labors; it is for their sakes that he sanctifies himself. As he looks at John and Mary and their fellows, there are several distinct tasks to which he commits himself on behalf of each one of them.

First of all, *he would like to round out their religious growth and experience.* Each of them has his own specific need—the place at which his own life is flat and incomplete instead of full-rounded. If the adult worker is on terms of friendly intimacy with the members of his group, he will know each of these points of need, bear it on his own heart, and try to meet it as opportunity arises. John is as good as gold, but he lacks self-confidence. Can we give him first a light responsibility and then a heavier one, bringing him into the foreground of the group's life by easy stages until he is eventually more sure of himself? Mary is highly talented, but badly spoiled and self-centered. Perhaps if her interest can be captured for our next service project, she will be brought face to face with pinched faces and pinched souls which will lift her out of her preoccupation with self. Ralph is the mainstay of the group's activities, into everything up to the hilt; but he has no devotional life worth the name. He is an activist, living merely on the surface of things. Perhaps a well-selected book would help him enter into a realm where he is as yet almost a stranger. Edith is faithful and able, but she absents herself consistently from our social affairs. What she needs more than anything else just now is a special invitation or an attractive responsibility for our next party.

And so the list goes, varying from one group to another and even from year to year in the same group. It is safe to say that an adult adviser has never known the full joy of his work until he has opened his eyes to individual needs of this sort and undertaken to meet them.

Secondly, *he would like to prepare his young people for service in the church.* As he summons them before his mind's eye one by one, he would like to see them someday not merely good, but good for something. Someday they must become the official board members, the church school teachers, the choir members, the recreational and dramatic leaders, the responsible heads of the auxiliaries of the church; and now is the time to begin their preparation for these tasks.

There is no better way of working toward this goal than through a wise handling of the many responsibilities now available in the young people's organization. Each person is to be helped patiently up the ladder from lesser to greater responsibilities as fast as he is willing and able to go—first membership on a committee perhaps, then a committee chairmanship, and finally the presidency of the group or some other major assignment. It is sheer satisfaction to watch them ascend and help them climb.

But beyond all this, full use needs to be made of such definite training opportunities as institutes, conventions, books, personal interviews, schools, and camps. These last have proved themselves so valuable that they deserve a separate word, which can best be given in the form of a remarkable report of one church's experience.

Some years ago we were faced with the problem of securing a trained leadership for our church school. In our desperation we turned to the training camps, and as an experiment sent two boys and four girls of high school age the first year.

The outcome was beyond our expectations, as all of them began to take an active part in the young people's department. The next year we sent twelve, and continued to increase the number until the peak year of 1930 we had fifty-four in training.

Since the depression and because our school is now supplied with an adequate teaching staff we fix our budget to allow for thirty-three each year. They are selected from the high school group according to a definite plan. Each teacher of this age is asked to furnish the principal of the department with the names of the three outstanding boys or girls in the class, as judged by their attendance, interest, and the like during the past nine months. The boys and girls selected are interviewed and, if agreeable all around, are then registered.

We finance this project in part by selling as many of these young people to the adult classes as we can. The person selected writes a letter of thanks to the class, and upon his return from camp attends a class meeting to express personally what the camp has meant to him. In this way we tie up the adult classes with the training program of youth, and it works.

Our school has eighty-six officers and teachers. From our camp-trained boys and girls we have the following now in active service: principal of the kindergarten department, assistant principal of the primary department, superintendent of the young people's division, principal of the intermediate department, principal of the young people's department, leader of the girls' choir, leader of our orchestra, leader of our League (and also a state officer), approximately twenty-five teachers and assistant teachers.

In the third place, *an adult worker with youth would like to give them individual counsel on their personal problems.* There are a limited number of youth workers who are able to render a personal counseling service to their young people which is virtually on the professional level. One minister, for example, assembles a set of data concerning each young person in his parish—records of interviews, the results of tests of vocational aptitude and emotional adjustment, the ratings of teachers, and the like. Through graduate study and long practical experience he has fitted himself for the difficult task of individual guidance. His young people are free to come to him at any time, but especially so during engagement, during the early marriage period, and during the choice of a life work.[3] A professional psychologist or psychiatrist could not do a great deal more than this. But most of us are not in a position to render such a service, and it might even be dangerous for us to try it. In this present discussion let us confine ourselves therefore to the personal counseling which can be done by anyone who genuinely cares for young people, and is willing to read, study, listen, and occasionally talk.

Anyone can be a true friend to youth. To do so requires no degrees in psychology. It does require certain qualities of personality which we do not all have, but which we can all cultivate little by little. And quite frequently what young people need most in the midst of their difficulties is merely the steadying assurance that they have a friend who cares for them and believes in them. This in itself may suffice to carry them through a rather severe crisis.

Anyone can listen. And very often all that young people need is merely the chance to pour out their troubles to someone who will not condemn nor become horrified, but will patiently listen. It is better, of course, if the counselor through a mastery of psychology can help the hard-beset youth to understand himself more fully. But if he can do no more than serve as a living sounding board against which the youth can talk to his heart's content, that is not to be despised.

Anyone can fit himself to be of some assistance in two of the most pressing problem areas of youth—namely, boy-girl relationships and the choice of a vocation. To become an expert counselor in these matters is, of course, the work of years. But anyone can achieve enough competency to be helpful if he will read open-mindedly some of the excellent books available. A few of the titles concerning boy-girl relationships have already been listed (in Chapter II). As a beginning on the vocational problem, the little booklet *Finding Your Work*[4] is both reliable and interesting. A winter's course of reading along these two lines will open up new and promising fields of helpfulness to any youth worker.

Anyone can equip himself to guide young people through some of their religious perplexities. All that is required is enough humility of soul to admit that other views than one's own may conceivably be right, plus the willingness to do some hard thinking and study. *Youth Looks at Religion* (previously referred to) would be a splendid start.

Anyone can open the way for young people to approach him on these and other problems. This "opening of the way" however must be done just so, or it will fall short of its purpose. It cannot be done with a professional flourish, and a blare of publicity. But sincere friendship will open the way. And a sympathetic, non-condemnatory attitude will open the way. And a clear knowledge of these subjects, as made evident in the programs of the entire group, will open the way very wide. Young people are most likely to consult in private the teacher or counselor who has in public demonstrated his interest and his competency in the problems that perplex them.

Anyone can show especial friendliness to a boy or girl who is obviously upset emotionally, and he can do so without attracting the curious attention of others. For example, a certain minister happened to know that a young man of his congregation was undergoing a period of unhappiness in his family life. He did not implore him to unburden himself, but invited him instead to be his companion in a day-long automobile trip. The unburdening took place quite naturally, as the minister anticipated it would. It is well to remember in this connection that frequently the young people who most need such special attention are the very ones of whom we would least suspect it—the quiet ones, the "good" ones, the faithful ones, and sometimes the ones who seem to be excessively happy but are in reality merely covering up a gnawing unhappiness.

These are some of the services that anyone can render, whether trained technically in psychology and personal counseling or not. This stress upon what all youth workers can do is not intended in the least to belittle psychology. That would be an unpardonable sin. Every youth worker owes it to those in his care to read as widely in general psychology, adolescent psychology, and personal counseling as his time permits and his previous education warrants.[5]

It would not be fair to leave this brief discussion of personal counseling without noting some of the grave dangers which beset it. There is the constant danger of handling a case unwisely, and leaving some young person worse off at the end than at the beginning. There is the danger of blossoming out into a self-appointed specialist in personal counseling, with the almost inevitable consequence of spoiling the natural relationship between the adult and his young people and rendering good counseling impossible. And there is, finally, the danger of enjoying counseling too much. It is altogether pleasant to be sought out by young people as a confidant. And it is doubly pleasant if the counselor, for example, happens to be a man and the counselee an attractive girl. These and other dangers will bear constant watching. The guidance of individual lives is not to be rushed into lightly—any more than a surgical operation. But the rewards far outweigh the dangers, great enough though they may be. Some of the best youth work must always be done by one and one. Christianity, it seems, has from the beginning been partial to the retail, rather than the wholesale, method.

SEVERAL FORGOTTEN MEN AMONG YOUTH

WE HEARD A GREAT deal in the recent depression years of "forgotten men." In church work too there are forgotten men. It is very hard for anyone to hold before his mind's eye all ages and all groups with absolute impartiality. Consequently, our attention from time to time gets focused upon some ages in particular, while out on the edge of our vision are other groups whom we see dimly or not at all. In youth work there would seem to be at the present moment three such forgotten men. Let us endeavor to make up for our partial neglect by looking squarely at each of them in turn for a little while.

THE INTERMEDIATE

By common consent the first forgotten man in church work with youth is the intermediate. (The term "junior high school" is fast supplanting "intermediate" as a designation for this twelve-thirteen-fourteen-year-old group.) We have lavished a good bit of attention on those just below him, and those just above him, but he himself has been frequently passed by. The juniors in all likelihood have a department of their own, and the seniors and young people have a society of their own, but he frequently has neither. He is too old for the children, and too young for the young people. He is "intermediate," betwixt and between, neither fish nor fowl

nor good red herring. To be sure, in some denominations
there is a church membership class provided especially for
him, but this meets for only a limited number of weeks and
affords little opportunity for social life and fellowship with
his own kind. A clear indication of the neglect he has
suffered is our failure to provide for his worship needs. There
are junior hymnals galore, and young people's hymnals, but
how many intermediate hymnals are there? While others
are caught up happily in programs well designed to fit their
needs and interests, he is frequently left to tag along as
best he can.

The truth of the matter, of course, is that he is a human
being with the same claim upon our time and our program
as any other human beings. During these very years he is
undergoing the rather bothersome changes of puberty, and
stands in considerable need of sympathetic care. Furthermore, this is the age of "joining the church" in many communions, and this significant fact gives him an additional and
peculiar claim upon our attention. With due apologies to
him for our neglect, let us endeavor to trace out a few of
the general principles which should govern us in constructing
a church program for the intermediate or junior high school
age.

1. *Intermediates need and deserve a separate place in the
church's organizational life.* If the congregation and its
building are large enough, there should by all means be an
intermediate department in the church school—of, by, and
for intermediates. If this is clearly out of the question, in
the congregation of medium size there can at least be two or
three classes of intermediates. The troublesome question
arises—a little more troublesome here than with older adoles-
cents—of whether to draw the line between these classes on

the basis of age or of sex. If the gossip and teasing to which many boys and girls are subjected has made them uncomfortable in one another's presence, or if the sexes have been separated in the lower departments, there may have to be a boys' class and a girls' class. In other cases the younger intermediates—boys and girls—can form one class, and the older intermediates another, inasmuch as there are some real differences not only in body but also in outlook upon life between a twelve-year-old and a fourteen-year-old. In such a case the younger class may be placed in the junior department, and the older class in the senior-young people's department. For the small church school the best that can be done may be simply a separate intermediate class with some social life and fellowship of its own.

2. *The most natural place for intermediates, generally speaking, is in the church school rather than in a Sunday evening intermediate society or fellowship.* This is a principle which is far-reaching, if true. The reasons for advancing it are two chiefly. In the first place, the fewer evening meetings intermediates have, the better—for health considerations primarily. Their junior high schools often make rather heavy demands upon them, and it is just as well if the church refrains from adding too much to the burdens they already have. Of course, a Sunday afternoon or an early Sunday evening program dodges this objection rather well. In the second place, intermediates seem to be most happy in a group of limited size. Professor Dimock found, for example, that the spontaneous neighborhood groups of the boys whom he studied had fourteen members each on the average.[1] The eighteen-year-old is very much at home in a group of twenty or thirty, but the intermediate seems to incline toward a smaller fellowship—something approximating

a gang or a club. This point, if true, argues in favor of the church school, with its traditional division into classes of about this size.

It would be dangerous to lay down the rule that always and everywhere work with intermediates is to be done through the church school. But it does seem safe to say that any additional ventures should be made only after the church school situation has been thoroughly canvassed and found wanting.

3. *Intermediates must have a good deal of activity in their program.* Boys and girls of this age have many accomplishments, but sitting motionless over long periods of time is not one of them. They must be active—if not in body, at least in mind and in voice. This is one reason why the programs of the Boy Scouts, the Girl Scouts, and the Camp Fire Girls appeal more strongly to the intermediate age; and it constitutes one good reason for the Church's wise utilization of these programs. And the implications for the Church's own program are unmistakable. There should be many activities in the literal sense of the word—hikes, games, some weekday meetings of church school classes, making and doing things with those intermediate hands that like the ocean are never still. Intermediates can be "active" in worship. There can be responses for the entire group, and singing, and participation under careful guidance in the leadership of the worship services. They can be active also in study. A recent booklet, *Church Work with the Junior High School Age,*[2] speaks of "Instruction Activities." This seems at first to be a queer phrase, almost paradoxical, but it is in truth a very good phrase. These intermediates can learn the geography of the Holy Land while they are actively engaged in making a relief map, and they can learn about the Church while

actively engaged in making a model of a church building, and they can learn many things while actively engaged in preparing and presenting dramas.[3] Some church schools have discovered that the problem of "discipline" with intermediate classes was almost solved by using the workbook type of lesson material—such as Courses VII, VIII, and IX of the Closely Graded Series. Perhaps one reason for the success of these workbooks is that they give boys and girls something to do with their hands.

If time seems all too short in the average school for activities of this sort, one obvious way out is an extended church school session—for the younger intermediates at least. An activity curriculum which would be unthinkable in one hour becomes easily possible in two.

4. *The intermediate program should bear in mind that in many denominations this is the age of entering into full church membership.* All of the plans which we lay may well be colored by this fact. If there is a church membership class alongside of the church school, these two should be correlated closely. The teachers and the pastor can consult with one another at regular intervals, in order to make sure that they are not working at cross purposes. The worship of the church school can embody some of the hymns, responses, and prayers of the church service by way of preparation for the church service itself. Some of the departmental worship sessions might be held in the church sanctuary with profit. The grading of the church school can take account of confirmation—or its equivalent—for instance, by making promotion from the intermediate to the senior department coincide with this significant step. And in particular the study curriculum of the church school can set as one of its chief aims the preparation of intermediates for

full church membership. The life of Christ, the history of the Christian Church, the history of the denomination and of the local church, private and corporate worship, what it means to follow Jesus—studies such as these belong naturally to the intermediate years.

THE YOUNG ADULT

Another forgotten man in youth work is the young adult. He is just as "intermediate," just as betwixt and between, just as forgotten as the junior high school age. He is too old for the youth group, and too young for the adult group.

In order to discover precisely how young adults feel concerning life in general and the church in particular, we may consult what they themselves have to say on such matters. Fifty of them were brought together several years ago in an informal conference. Their findings were reported as follows:

PROBLEMS EXPRESSED BY THE GROUP

Influence of beverage alcohol on home life.
The hopelessness of this generation.
How can we make a living today?
We need guidance for our leisure time.
What is a Christian home?
War and international relations make life unchristian.
I can't find a place in my church.
Present organizations give no satisfying worship experience.
I need help in building a philosophy of life.
Citizenship means little.
I can't find my place in a social group.
There is no transition group from youth to adult life in the church.
I need help in fitting myself into new environments.

CRITERIA ADVANCED FOR IDENTIFYING YOUNG ADULTS

The end of formal education.
Marriage.
Economic independence.
Leaving the parental home.
Moving out of the environment of childhood.

REASONS GIVEN FOR DRIFTING FROM THE CHURCH

Lack of a vital program for young adults; no social life; no opportunity for participation; one person does all the talking.
Failure of the church to set up a definite cause or purpose.
Dominance of the older conservatives in church program building.
Real practical Christianity not much in evidence.
Church has no convictions on current issues.

It would not be true to say that the Church is wholly indifferent to these young adults and the dilemmas in which they find themselves. Indeed the past few years have seen considerable remembering of this forgotten man. Conferences have been held, plans laid, and several books and booklets published with the phrase "young adults" in the title. In this newly found work what are the chief principles which should guide our efforts?

1. *Young adults deserve a separate place in the church's organizational life.* We do not have in mind here a separate church school department—as was the case with intermediates—but rather a separate class, or guild, or league, or fellowship, of, by, and for young adults. There may be some churches so small that this cannot be done; but in most of them it is possible, and very necessary. As a matter of fact, young adult organizations are springing up in every section of the country. Some of them meet on Sunday morning, some on Sunday evening, and some on week nights. Some

of them include both the married and the unmarried, but a good many of them are for couples only—married couples. In a few large churches there may be four or five distinct young adult groups. These new organizations display real ingenuity in finding or inventing names. Yomaco (young married couples) Club, Fireside Club, G. G. and G. Club (meaning unknown to outsiders), Mariners' Club (the good ship "Matrimony," of course), and Kill Kare Klub are among the most alluring.[4] The Triangle Club (father, mother, and the baby) is a true "natural" as a designation for parents' groups.

Organizations such as these will in some instances be launched quite informally. In one church the minister announced a social evening for all those twenty-five to forty. A great deal of fun was had in hurling dire threats at any under twenty-five or over forty who should dare to come, and a good time was had by all when the evening arrived. It would be easy on such an occasion to propose that "we get together again soon," and thus take the first step toward definite organization.

2. *The program of these young adult organizations may have to be somewhat unconventional.* It need not be bizarre or spectacular, but on the other hand it must not fall into one of the old familiar ruts of church work. Perhaps the safest rule is to make much of sheer fellowship at the outset, and when a close group life has been developed let the program grow out of that as it will. At first it may have little to do with religion in the narrow sense of the word—particularly if some of the young adults have been out of touch with the church for a while—but time will in all likelihood change that. Apparently a number of these organizations have run about the same course—namely, beginning with

mere sociability and a discussion perhaps of community problems, and drawing nearer by stages to the church and its traditional interests until finally worship and church attendance have a place in their life which would have been unthinkable at the start.

3. *When young adults do join with others for any purpose,
their most natural affinity is with adults rather than young
people.* After all, young adults are not older youth; they are
young adults. When they join with others in a church school
department, or for worship of any sort, or for fellowship, the
direction in which they should turn in most cases would
seem to be toward the adults rather than toward the young
people.

4. *Adult groups can ease the transition of young adults
into their ranks materially by a wise adjustment of their own
program.* If young adults do not always feel at home in
adult groups, it is not primarily because of any lack of cor-
diality among their elders. It is rather that the program is
so different from what they have known in their youth fellowships. They may have been accustomed to a great deal
of heated discussion; and they are asked now to keep still
and listen. They may have been used to a rather free
choice of their own curriculum; they find now perhaps a
rigid adherence to the International Uniform Lessons. They
may have been members of an active, vigorous group which
"went places and did things"; they find themselves now in
a more easy-going and sedate company. Their chief concern during past years may have been the application of the
gospel to social issues; they discover now a gospel for individuals one by one and a strange silence concerning war and
peace, economics, and the racial question.

This is not to suggest that the situation in every church is as depicted here. But on the whole a different type of program, a different emphasis, a different approach have prevailed in youth work from those in vogue among adults. If young adults, then, do not seem altogether at home in adult groups, they need more than a hearty slap on the back by a member of the welcoming committee. Nothing short of some fundamental readjustments of the program will turn the trick.

It would be too much to ask of adults that they overhaul their programs completely just to please these recruits. But they can make some changes in the direction, for example, of more discussion and a more flexible curriculum both to their own good and to the good of the newcomers. Beyond this, by sharing offices and committee responsibilities with the incoming generation of adults, they can afford them opportunity for a full exercise of their abundant energy and initiative.

The Student

The third forgotten man among youth is the student, particularly the student who is away from home at college or university or nursing or business school. Something is happening today which never happened before in world history. Thousands of our best and brainiest young men and women are being lifted out of their home churches and communities around the age of eighteen and sent elsewhere for four years or more. The chances are that they entered into full church membership only three or four years previously. They are now at the point where they could begin to render a fine service as teachers and officers in the church. They need the ministrations of religion greatly. And at this very moment we tear them up by the roots and forcibly transplant them to other soil. Here they come face to face in all probability with teachers and ideas and ways of life that unsettle them. The ties with the home church become weaker and weaker. They can attend its services only in summer and on holidays, and that is not enough to keep interest and loyalty fully alive. As for the churches in the college community, the students may or may not find their way into one of them. And so they "sit down between two chairs." Never before did this sort of thing happen on so large a scale. Those who will be the leaders of our national life and could be the leaders of our religious life are suffering a rude interruption of their church affiliations just as they are growing into manhood and womanhood.

It would not be true to the facts to paint this picture in colors that are too dark. There are many college students to whom religion means a great deal. One careful study reveals more than half of the college students surveyed thinking well of the church and inclined favorably toward it.[5] There is here no cause for wide alarm. The record of the average members of the average church might not be a great deal better.

On the other hand, the evidence is rather clear that the church attendance of college students does fall off to a considerable degree. We have one most interesting comparison between the church participation of some young people during the months before going to college and their participation during the months after their arrival. Beforehand, about three-fourths of them went to church frequently, and almost half took part in various organizations within the church. In college, these figures fell to 43 per cent and 18 per cent respectively.[6] If this same decline were to happen annually with an equal number of other youth, we would be horrified. For some reason or other we manage to accept it with some complacency in the case of college youth.

The problem of the college student can be attacked from two vantage points: the college and college community on the one hand, and the home church on the other. The attack from the college end is not our primary concern in this connection. Suffice it to say that whatever is done from that angle will have to be done both at church-related colleges and at tax-supported institutions. (A certain denomination which is proud of its educational heritage discovered several years ago that 146 of its own young people were enrolled at one of its oldest and best colleges, while 273 of them were in the student body of a tax-supported institution a hundred miles distant.) But our present concern is with the attack upon the problem from the vantage point of the local church. What can a home church do to keep the religious life of its young people intact during their student days? It would seem that there are three general answers to this question, and only three.

1. *It can keep its contact with them unbroken during the months they are away at school.* This may require a good many postage stamps, but it is worth it. Personal letters and remembrances, church bulletins, denominational journals, denominational youth papers, manuals of private devotion, special announcements of home church events—all of these will help to keep the ties unbroken between the absentee student and his church. This is a task for youth groups, for pastors, and for the denomination as a whole. A youth fellowship might well have a committee to keep in touch with members away at school. The pastor, among other things, can send the names of his young people religiously

to pastors in the college communities where they are going, in order that a new association may be set up at once. One denomination issues a special student edition of its youth magazine every few months, and sends copies free of charge to all the young people of its fellowship who are in college and whose names have been supplied by their pastors. Other denominations accomplish the same purpose in other ways. All of these together constitute what might be called a correspondence course in church loyalty.

2. *It can make the most of the summer months and the vacation periods when the students are at home.* Before they leave in the fall, there is a place for special parties, and special services, and prayers offered on their behalf in the corporate worship of the congregation, and their names in print in the church bulletin. If this becomes morbidly sentimental, it will of course have only the effect of embarrassing and repelling these youth, but it need not become so. And when they return at Christmas or Easter or in early summer, there may be a communion service for them in particular, or a youth program in which they are given a prominent part. During the summer months ways need to be sought out for catching them up quickly once more in the life and work of the church. Assistant teachers in the church school are often needed at this time, and room may be found for them in committees of the youth fellowship. In such ways they can be helped to pick up the threads of church activity which were severed some months before.

3. *Most important of all, the home church can do its level best to provide them in advance with a religious faith of such strength and quality that it will stand the test of the student years.* In other words, the time to solve the problem of holding college youth to the church and religion is five to ten

years before they leave for college. In support of this statement, we refer once more to the comparative study of the religious experience of students before and after going away to school. It is clearly stated in the report of this study that the attitude of the student toward religion in his precollege days has much to do with the degree of his religious participation in college. If religion meant much to him beforehand, he tends to continue his church interests and activities in the college community. And on a later page it is further stated that those who attended church regularly before college tend to persist in this practice during college; it is those who attended none too regularly beforehand who are most likely to fall away in college.[7]

From another point of view also this appears to be true. It used to be that the first blow to childhood religious faith came in college, but this is no longer fully the case. The scientific temper has now thoroughly saturated our high schools, and it may be that the testing time now begins some years earlier than was formerly the case. At least this is the conclusion suggested by the life histories of a number of college students who had lost faith, or a good part of it. In a study of almost four hundred students, 178 of them were found to be far over to the left in their religious beliefs— not holding to faith either in a personal God or in individual immortality as a rule. The question was then raised, When and where did this begin? Where did these students lose religion? It appeared that in 69 per cent of these cases the chief step in this direction was made not during the college but during the high school years.[8] Such a state of affairs would have been impossible a generation ago, but it is all too possible today.

All of this evidence converges on the conclusion that the

finest service a home church can render a college student falls not after but before he leaves for college. If it can help him to cultivate a religious faith of the proper *strength* and *quality*—both words are essential—beforehand, it can breathe more easily when he packs his trunk and begins his student days away from home. His religious faith must be strong. If he attends church regularly and takes part in its program actively, if he majors in religion as it were, he is likely to maintain his religious interest throughout the college years. But his Christian faith must also have a certain quality. Specifically, it needs to be as free from all superstitious and unscientific elements as possible. The core of Christian truth has not been shaken by science or philosophy in the least— that is, our basic convictions concerning the goodness and the power and the wise purpose of the God whose face we have seen in Jesus Christ. But there are particular types of Christian doctrine which a high school or college teacher who wants to do so can riddle rather effectively. So long, therefore, as we cause our young people's faith to rest upon views of the Bible or of creation or of miracle or of Jesus himself which are clearly untenable in the light of modern science, we can expect nothing else than a loss of faith on the part of some of our youth.

There are, then, these three ways in which a home church can act to hold its college youth steadfast; and the greatest of these is the last.

X

BEYOND THE LOCAL CHURCH

OUR PRIMARY CONCERN in church work with youth must ever be the program within the local congregation. But while youth work must begin in the local church, it dare not stop there.

WITHIN THE DENOMINATION

For some reason or other the past few years have been marked by an irresistible upsurge of denominational interest in youth. Some communions, of course, have had well-defined youth programs for many years; but others, which have never known a denomination-wide youth fellowship, have been busy forming them of late. Perhaps this new development is part and parcel of a general awakening to the possibilities resident within Christian education. At all events, it has happened.

Clearly discernible within these ventures is a rather marked trend in the direction of a denomination-wide youth *fellowship* rather than a denomination-wide *organization*. There is a real difference between these two words and what they severally stand for, and each has its own peculiar advantages. The organization type has the advantage of greater definiteness. It prescribes a definite pattern for each local youth group—a definite set of officers, a definite constitution, a definite program. The fellowship type, on the other hand, is more flexible, more adaptable to varying local conditions. It strives to catch up youth groups of whatever sort seems best in any given case—classes, societies, guilds, leagues—into one wide fellowship, and then within that fellowship to provide guidance and inspiration for all. If we were to chart the fellowship type of denominational youth program, it might appear somewhat like the following:

1. *Within the local church—*
   a) The type of youth organization and program which best suits each particular situation.
   b) Clear-cut guidance supplied from denominational headquarters in the form of a concrete description of the various types with their respective advantages and disadvantages.
2. *Within each area—conference, synod, or association—*
   a) An area youth fellowship, bound together by the following ties:
   b) A youth assembly or conference for the area, held at least annually.
   c) An area cabinet elected at this annual assembly, composed two-thirds of youth and one-third of adult counselors of youth.
   d) Joint work on a common project or projects, such as the support of student work at a denominational college within the area.
   e) Where the area is large, occasional meetings for the youth of subareas.
   f) Perhaps a mimeographed news sheet or journal.
3. *Within the denomination—*
   a) A denominational youth fellowship, bound together by the following ties:
   b) A youth assembly for the entire denomination, held every three or four years.
   c) A denominational youth cabinet—two-thirds young people and one-third adult counselors—elected at this

assembly, or else composed of representatives from the area fellowships.

d) Joint work on a common project or projects, such as the support of a mission school or several youth within it.

e) A denominational youth journal.

f) Programs for common worship and study, which are suggestive but not obligatory.

g) A common purpose to which each local group is invited to subscribe, receiving in return a certificate of affiliation.

Several of the items in such a scheme are worthy of note. One is the democracy of it. It is truly democratic, yet not anarchic. It proceeds from below up, yet with guidance from above down. Another is the absence of any mention of dues or other financial payments from the smaller to the larger unit. In lieu of these—or at least alongside of them— it is expected that each young person as a member of his own church will give financial support to the entire program of the denomination, a part of which is the board of Christian education, and a part of which in turn is the youth work of the denomination. This plan has the great merit of attaching young people to the church as a whole, rather than merely their own little corner of it. It is calculated to make churchmen and churchwomen—not narrow-visioned devotees of a youth organization.

Such in brief is the form which denominational youth organizations are assuming more and more. Further details concerning the way in which a plan of this sort has actually worked out in one denomination are to be found in a bulletin entitled *What Is the Pilgrim Fellowship?* [1]

INTERDENOMINATIONAL

One of the brightest pages in the story of interdenominational co-operation has been written by the forces of Christian education. If people of the several communions are today more willing to work together and to recognize one another as fellow Christians than they were fifty years ago, this result is traceable in no small part to the long and persistent fellowship across denominational lines which workers in Christian education have maintained for more than a century.

It comes with a shock, therefore, to realize that in our own day there is a decided trend within Christian education in the direction of denominationalism. It is not that interdenominationalism has been given up, but merely that denominationalism is being stressed. All along the Christian education line—youth work included—there is this stirring of new life within many communions. It requires no special prophetic gifts to detect herein a potential dagger thrust at the very heart of our interdenominational work. The multiplication of denominational youth camps contains an implied threat to the interdenominational camps. The scheduling of denominational youth conferences may make the task of securing delegates for interdenominational conferences more and more difficult. The vigorous prosecution of denominational youth programs promises, in short, to drain off into new channels some of the interest and energy which have hitherto been devoted to interdenominational programs. After all, there are only so many days in each year and only so much energy in each person, and what is taken by this cannot be given to that.

Because of this trend which is upon us, it is imperative in our day that we plan deliberately to maintain unbroken fellowship of Christian youth across denominational barriers. It would be both tragic and ironical if, at the very moment when the word "ecumenical" is upon everybody's lips, we should in our youth work build high again the ancient and ugly walls which separate groups of Christians from each other. We must hold steadily before our eyes the abiding values of interdenominational youth work—the common approach to common problems, the support of the weak by the strong, and the enrichment of each out of the heritage of all. We dare not let co-operative youth work languish and die.

One of the oldest and most extensive interdenominational ventures in youth fellowship is that which has been sponsored over many years by the various levels of Sunday School Associations—district, county, nation, and world. The nature and value of this interdenominational program are apparent in the following report from a county young people's superintendent within an eastern state:

Many years ago the Sabbath School Association divided our county into eleven districts. It has been my constant aim to have a young people's council in each district. Thus far we have ten of the eleven districts organized.

The general membership of the council is made up of any young people who wish to come from all of the churches in the district. Each council meets regularly once a month on a specific night, such as the last Tuesday night of the month, or the first Monday. We meet at the various churches on a rotating schedule. During the summer, however, we hold outdoor meetings at well-chosen spots in the several communities.

In order to keep the county work more or less unified, share ideas, find out one another's needs, and build a program to fit them, we have the superintendent and officers of each district meet together with the county officers and superintendents quarterly. This group we call our County Young People's Council.

Another young people's superintendent, writing from a

county where a program of this sort has been in existence for a quarter of a century, bears his testimony in the following words:

We have seen the Christian youth of our communities drawn closer together in fellowship and sympathy. We have seen a constant stream of leadership being trained through the interdenominational work, and going back into their own churches to enrich the work there. We have seen the council assisting local churches to work out their youth programs and reach their denominational standards. We have seen entire communities coming together for Easter dawn services, Christmas caroling, and other meetings of this type under council guidance. We have seen campaigns organized and conducted under council leadership for China relief and similar causes. In short, there seems to be no limit to the possibilities if we are given an earnest and effective leadership.

There is evident vitality in programs such as these. Something is happening, and something good. They deserve by all means to be continued, and to be developed still further. But in what directions should they develop?

1. *We are already witnessing a change in geography*—from the district as a unit to the county or community as a unit. The division of counties into districts was admirable when it was first made—the horse-and-buggy days when a trip of more than three or four miles was nothing short of an undertaking. But good roads and the automobile have changed many things, and they are fast altering this too. We are therefore undergoing a shift toward more natural units— either an entire county, or else a town with the surrounding countryside of which it is the cultural center.

2. *We are witnessing likewise a change in representation*— from the local church as a basis to the organized youth agen-

cies within a county or community. Here, for example, in a given locality are the area organization of Christian Endeavor, and the Y.M.C.A., and the Y.W.C.A., and perhaps ten or twelve denominations. All of these are actively engaged in youth work—now! All of them have programs which are going concerns. When we come to promote an interdenominational fellowship of Christian youth, why should we not constitute it out of these agencies? The chief gain to accrue is that the interdenominational fellowship then coordinates the programs which are already in running order, instead of setting up yet another program in addition to and in competition with those previously in the field. This plan raises some problems in the field of finance, but they are not too formidable.

3. *We are witnessing further a change in function*—from the mere stimulation of work in local youth groups to this plus the performance of Christian tasks which belong to all alike and can be done best by all together. The raising of funds for China relief is such a task; campaigning against obscene literature is another; and the encouragement of liquorless eating places yet another. The Christian youth of a county or community could render a signal service to the young people of their area by broadcasting—either literally or figuratively—evaluations of motion pictures currently being shown. If they live in a locality of many migrant youth, or many unemployed youth, they would not have to search long for a common task. If there is a college within their area, they might attempt to reach the student population for associate membership in churches and youth fellowships within the college community. In directions such as these our interdenominational youth organizations can ex-

pand the scope of their work with equal benefit to their communities and themselves.

INTERFAITH AND INTERRACE

Interdenominational fellowship of Christian youth is all to the good, so far as it goes; but it does not go far enough. It still leaves "beyond the pale" two sizable groups of American youth, the Roman Catholics and the Jews. It also fails to make a sure place for all of those eager and capable youth who do not happen to be white-skinned. In a day when the smoldering coals of prejudice are being fanned into searing flames of bitter hatred throughout the world, we must double and redouble the opportunities for friendly contact across the lines of "race and clan." Of all the challenges which reach Protestant youth today, are there any more urgent than this one?

As living evidence of what can be done, an excursion into this field may be described briefly. It is an interracial fellowship of white and Negro youth in one of our largest American cities. Through the years a considerable Negro infiltration has been added to the predominantly white population of this city, until the tension between the two mounted high at times. About ten years ago eighty young people of both races were called together in a conference to see what could be done to relieve this tension, and cultivate mutual sympathy and appreciation in its stead. The result was the organization of a Young People's Interracial Fellowship which has done untold good within the city itself, and furnished inspiration to many others in near and distant places. The life and work of the Fellowship is thus described by one who has been closely identified with it since its inception:

What a record of varied activities the young people of the Interracial Fellowship have written these eight years! They have gone out by twos, in apostolic fashion, to tell the story of inter-racial fraternity in churches, clubs, and schools. They have called together ministers, church school workers, and officers of youth organizations to explore what the local church could do to establish friendship and justice between the races. They have prepared exhibits of Negro achievements in art, music, and literature. Every month from October to April for the last four years they have conducted monthly services of their Fellowship Church at 3:45 o'clock of a Sunday afternoon. There are two ministers, one Negro, one white. The choir and the congregation are made up of people of both races. Thus in the presence of God we celebrate the unity of Christian believers, the oneness of humanity. One hundred and forty of them went together to see *The Green Pastures* when Richard Harrison brought his company to our city. After the play, they went backstage and shook hands with De Lawd himself, and with his angel, Gabriel. There have been other theater parties since that time. The group has carried on serious studies of the relation between race and housing, health, education, and culture. They have under-taken to develop enlightened Christian attitudes concerning Jews and their proper status in a democracy. They have called mass meetings against lynching. They have listened to the story of the sharecroppers. Some of the members have worked to eliminate the discriminations against Negroes which are the accepted practice in hospitals, theaters, restaurants, and churches. And through the years, month by month, these young people have met around supper tables, looked into each other's eyes, and dis-covered for themselves that fellowship is better than division, association better than segregation.

COMMUNITY PLANNING FOR YOUTH

A community might be defined as a number of people living in a given area and possessing many interests in com-mon. Quite naturally, therefore, they organize to care for these common interests. Among all the concerns which the people of a community hold in common, are there any more precious than the community's youth? It would seem, then, the most natural thing in the world that the people of a community should organize in some way or other to safeguard the life and health, both physical and spiritual, of their young people. Happily there is a fresh development in this direction at the present time. From coast to coast communities are marshaling their resources in the interests of their youth—not all of them, nor even most of them, but enough of them to raise hopes for the future.

As an illustration of this trend, we may take the story of a midwestern city of about 12,500 population.[2] This city had youth and it had youth problems, but it did not open its eyes clearly to either till the depression struck like an unexpected cyclone some ten years ago. As it surveyed the human wreckage which resulted, it gathered up its resolution, its ideas, and its money, and set to work. The first step was to lay a recreation tax to supply the needed funds. The next step was to secure permission from the Board of Education to make use of an outmoded school building for club meetings, as well as the gymnasiums and playgrounds of the school system after hours. The third step was to organize a Foundation for Youth, which would solicit the support of individuals and community organizations, and carry out the completed program. A man skilled in recreational supervision was employed to devote his time to the project. A boys' club was organized for youth of all ages, beginning at nine and stopping at adulthood. The club's schedule of activities included a variety of athletic teams, hobby groups, and special parties. The membership grew from 289 at the outset to 1,046 at the time this report was written.   The latter figure represents about three-fourths of the 'teen-age boys of the community.   Little by little the program reached out to include girls also, with the eventual organization of a girls' club in another out-of-date school building—not to mention quite a few coeducational activities. In due time a camp site was donated, and a part of the Foundation's program moved out of doors.   This site has gradually been improved through gifts from individuals and civic clubs and some federal assistance, until now half of the city's youth can go to camp each summer in the city's camp. The total annual cost of this entire program is about $15,000, which is a good bit less than the expense of maintaining a decent jail for a year.   That is what one community has done.

So far as one can judge, the churches of this community had little part as such in this splendid undertaking.   Perhaps they could not have done otherwise, the setup of the plan being what it was.   However, all of us who are devoted to the Church cannot help being jealous of the Church's role in community plans for youth.   Fortunately, there is a type of community organization on behalf of youth which makes a place for churches alongside of schools, civic clubs, parent-teacher organizations, lodges, and the like.   The form of organization which accomplishes this happy result is the Co-ordinating Council, in which all the significant units of a community's life through their chosen representatives join in the great task of serving the highest interests of youth.   Many communities have formed these "spiritual chambers of commerce"—to their lasting benefit.   The story of their achievements, as well as of many other efforts at community planning for youth, is to be found in a significant bulletin prepared by the Committee on Youth Problems in the Office of Education of our federal government.[3]

And so our consideration of youth work in the church draws to a close. In all that has been said, and in all that remains to be done, there is one abiding center around which all else revolves—youth itself. Our Lord on one occasion set a little child in the midst of a company. There were parents in that company, and those who were to become the first church fathers; but a little child was at the center. What he did, we too must do. In the midst of our thinking and planning we must set youth itself—not to be catered to obsequiously, but to be served in the spirit of Jesus and to be built up in our most holy faith. If we render this service faithfully and well, we may dare to hope that other needful things will be added unto us: the strengthening of the Church, the redeeming of our communities, the safeguarding of our national life, and someday the dawning of that kingdom of righteousness and peace, of faith and of love, which is our heart's desire.

NOTES AND REFERENCES

CHAPTER I: YOUTH CONFRONTS THE CHURCH

1. *Sermons for the Times.*
2. Dimock, *Rediscovering the Adolescent,* Association Press, 1937, pp. 24-25.
3. *Ibid.,* p. 162.
4. *Ibid.,* p. 169.
5. *Ibid.,* pp. 28-30.
6. *Ibid.,* p. 277.
7. *The Annals of the American Academy of Political and Social Science,* November, 1937, p. 7.
8. H. P. Rainey et al., *How Fare American Youth?* D. Appleton-Century Co., 1938, p. 4.
9. *The Annals of the American Academy of Political and Social Science,* November, 1937, p. 7.
10. *Ibid.,* p 15.
11. *Ibid.,* p. 10.
12. *Ibid.,* p. 27.
13. *Ibid.,* p. 1.   Reprinted by permission.
14. H. M. Bell, *Youth Tell Their Story,* American Council on Education, 1938, p. 105.
15. *The Annals of the American Academy of Political and Social Science,* November, 1937, p. 20.
16. Rainey, *op. cit.,* p. 22.
17. Bell, *op. cit.,* p. 250.
18. Rainey, *op. cit.,* p. 29.
19. *Ibid.,* p. 27.
20. *Ibid.,* p. 139.
21. *Ibid.,* p. 141.

22. R. A. Burkhart, *Understanding Youth,* Abingdon Press, 1938, p. 23.
23. Rainey, *op. cit.,* p. 79.
24. *Ibid.,* pp. 80-81.
25. Bell, *op. cit.,* p. 168.
26. Rainey, *op. cit.,* p. 157.
27. *Ibid.,* pp. 159-160.
28. *The Annals of the American Academy of Political and Social Science,* November, 1937, p. 80.
29. Burkhart, *op. cit.,* p. 21.
30. *Ibid.,* p. 40.
31. *Ibid.,* p. 26.
32. Rainey, *op. cit.,* p. 167.   Reprinted by permission.
33. *Ibid.,* p. 167.
34. Bell, *op. cit.,* p. 205.
35. *Ibid.,* p. 196.
36. *Ibid.,* p. 198.
37. *The Annals of the American Academy of Political and Social Science,* November, 1937, p. 54.
38. Burkhart, *op. cit.,* p. 48.
39. *Ibid.,* p. 47.
40. A. R. Gilliland, "How Religious Is the College Student?" in *International Journal of Religious Education,* May, 1939, pp. 20 f.
41. Letter by J. C. Baker in *The Christian Century,* July 1, 1936, p. 929.   Reprinted by permission.

CHAPTER II: SIX BASIC NEEDS OF YOUTH

1. Reported in *The Epworth Herald,* April 6, 1940, p. 2.
2. An admirable choice would be A. C. Wickenden, *Youth Looks at Religion,* Harper & Bros., 1939.   The Hazen Series also contains some excellent small books for this purpose.
3. *The Upper Room,* Nashville, Tenn.
4. Bell, *op. cit.,* p. 74.
5. *Ibid.,* p. 75.
6. *Ibid.,* pp. 131-133.

7. V. Rhein, "Finding Ourselves," in *International Journal of Religious Education*, October, 1939, pp. 6 f.

8. Bell, *op cit.*, p. 40.

9. O. M. Butterfield, *Love Problems of Adolescence*, Emerson Books, Inc., 1939, p. 182.

10. R. A. Burkhart, *From Friendship to Marriage*, Harper & Bros., 1937, pp. 60-61.

11. T. G. Soares, *Religious Education*, University of Chicago Press, 1928, p. 267.

CHAPTER III: THE PLACE OF YOUTH IN THE CHURCH

1. Burkhart, *Understanding Youth*, pp. 131-136.

2. "Is Youth in the Church?" in *International Journal of Religious Education*, April, 1929, p. 5. Used by permission.

3. *The Epworth Herald*, May 18, 1940, p. 2.

4. *Ibid.*, June 15, 1940, p. 2.

5. J. R. Hargreaves, " 'A Next Step' in Rural Religious Effort," in *Religious Education*, 1932, pp. 363 ff.

6. P. R. and M. H. Hayward, *Getting Along Together*, Westminster Press, 1940.

CHAPTER IV: YOUTH AND THE CHURCH SERVICE

1. Burkhart, *Understanding Youth*, p. 124.

2. *The Epworth Herald*, April 20, 1940, p. 28.

3. D. C. Wilson, Walter H. Baker Co.

4. Reported by R. L. Folk in *Reformed Church Messenger*, January 17, 1935, pp. 7-8.

5. S. A. Weston, editor, *Sermons I Have Preached to Young People*, Pilgrim Press, 1932. Used by permission.

6. J. R. Lyons, "Youth and Pastor in Co-operative Sermonizing," in *International Journal of Religious Education*, March, 1931, p. 26.

CHAPTER V: YOUTH AND THE CHURCH SCHOOL

1. Burkhart, *Understanding Youth*, p. 150.

2. "The Church School Closely Graded Courses," prepared by

The Graded Press. The material can be obtained from most denominational supply houses.

3. The idea of such a list as this came in the first instance from Erwin L. Shaver; he is not to be held responsible, however, for the content here given.

4. International Council of Religious Education, 203 N. Wabash Ave., Chicago, Ill., or denominational supply houses.

5. *Idem.*

6. H. P. Douglass and E. deS. Brunner, *The Protestant Church as a Social Institution,* Harper & Bros., 1935, p. 160.

CHAPTER VI: THE YOUTH SOCIETY OR FELLOWSHIP

1. *The Society Quarterly,* Westminster Press (Presbyterian U. S. A.), Witherspoon Building, Philadelphia, Pa.

2. Published by Abingdon Press. Available through most denominational supply houses.

3. 14 Beacon St., Boston, Mass.

4. International Council of Religious Education, or denominational supply houses.

5. P. C. Landers, "The University of Life: A New Type of Sunday Evening Youth Program," in *International Journal of Religious Education,* January, 1939, pp. 6 f.

6. Reported orally by R. A. Burkhart.

CHAPTER VII: METHODS OF WORK WITH YOUTH

1. Available in *The Church School Hymnal for Youth,* Westminster Press, 1931, pp. 395-396.

2. Reported by E. M. Dawe in *Youth,* April 21, 1940, p. 16.

3. Substantially this order was suggested by R. W. Schloerb in 1921 in a thesis, *The Meaning and Function of Worship in American Protestantism.*

4. For example, these two recent ones: A. A. Bays, *Worship Programs in the Fine Arts,* Abingdon Press, 1940; J. G. Howard, *When Youth Worships,* Bethany Press, 1940.

5. It was Professor C. D. Spotts who formulated the matter in this fashion.

6. These suggestions had their origin in a series drafted by Professor Goodwin Watson, and any usefulness they may have is partly to be credited to his account. See G. Watson and R. B. Spence, *Educational Problems for Psychological Study*, Macmillan Co., 1930, pp. 336-339.

7. Bell, *op. cit.*, pp. 161-162.

8. *Ibid.*, p. 181.

9. See, e.g., K. L. Heaton, *Character Building Through Recreation*, University of Chicago Press, 1929, pp. 60-62.

10. Reported by Mrs. E. F. Wilson in *Youth*, June 23, 1940, p. 13.

11. N. E. Richardson, *The Church at Play*, The Abingdon Press, 1922, pp. 114-116.

12. L. G. Deseo and H. M. Phipps, Abingdon Press, 1931.

13. M. M. Russell, *Producing Your Own Plays*, Richard R. Smith, 1931.

14. Most denominational supply houses can furnish several such lists.

CHAPTER VIII. THE WORKER HIMSELF

1. Burkhart, *Understanding Youth*, pp. 140-141.

2. G. Watson, "Democracy Makes People Different," in *The Epworth Herald*, May 18, 1940, pp. 5 f.

3. Burkhart, *Understanding Youth*, p. 145.

4. J. G. White, Association Press, 1938.

5. E.g., R. A. Burkhart, *Guiding Individual Growth*, Abingdon Press, 1935.

CHAPTER IX: SEVERAL FORGOTTEN MEN AMONG YOUTH

1. Dimock, *op. cit.*, p. 187.

2. Presbyterian Board of Christian Education, 1940.

3. See, e.g., H. Niebuhr, *Ventures in Dramatics*, Chas. Scribner's Sons, 1935.

4. *Young Adults in the Church*, International Council of Religious Education, 1939, pp. 11-16.

5. H. Hartshorne, editor, *From School to College*, Yale University Press, 1939, p. 284.

6. *Ibid.,* pp. 52, 253.
7. *Ibid.,* pp. 253, 264.
8. M. C. T. Van Tuyl, "Where Do Students Lose Religion?" in *Religious Education,* January-March, 1939, pp. 19 ff.

CHAPTER X: BEYOND THE LOCAL CHURCH

1. Congregational Publishing Society, 14 Beacon St., Boston, Mass.
2. *New Strength for America,* American Youth Commission of the American Council on Education, 1940.
3. *Youth . . . . How Communities Can Help,* U. S. Government Printing Office, 1936.